ISBN 978-1-331-38494-6
PIBN 10182735

This book is a reproduction of an important historical work. Forgotten Books uses
state-of-the-art technology to digitally reconstruct the work, preserving the original format
whilst repairing imperfections present in the aged copy. In rare cases, an imperfection in
the original, such as a blemish or missing page, may be replicated in our edition. We do,
however, repair the vast majority of imperfections successfully; any imperfections that
remain are intentionally left to preserve the state of such historical works.

1 MONTH OF
FREE
READING

at

www.ForgottenBooks.com

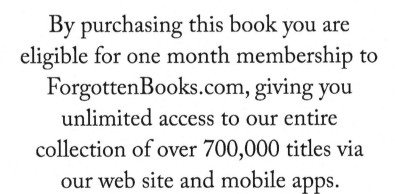

By purchasing this book you are
eligible for one month membership to
ForgottenBooks.com, giving you
unlimited access to our entire
collection of over 700,000 titles via
our web site and mobile apps.

To claim your free month visit:

www.forgottenbooks.com/free182735

INTRODUCTION.

———————

THE following Poems will probably attract some notice by their intrinsic merit; but they are also entitled to attention from the circumstances under which they were written. They are the genuine productions of a young Peasant, a day-labourer in husbandry, who has had no advantages of education beyond others of his class; and though Poets in this country have seldom been fortunate men, yet he is, perhaps, the least favoured by circumstances, and the most destitute of friends, of any that ever existed.

JOHN CLARE, the author of this Volume, was born at Helpstone, near Peterborough, Northamptonshire, on the 13th of July, 1793. He is the only son of Parker and Ann Clare, who are also natives of the same village, where they have always resided in extreme poverty; nor are they aware that any of their ancestors have been in better circumstances. Parker Clare is a farmer's labourer, and latterly he was employed in threshing; but violent colds brought on the rheumatism to such a degree that he was at length unable to work, or even to move without assistance. By the kind liberality of Lord Milton he was then sent to the Sea-bathing Infirmary at Scarborough, where he found great relief; but returning home part of the way on foot, from a desire to save expenses, his exertions and exposure to the weather brought on the pain again, and reduced him to a more deplorable state than ever. He is now a helpless cripple, and a pauper, receiving an allowance of five shillings a week from the parish.

JOHN CLARE has always lived with his parents at Helpstone, except for those short periods when the distance to which he was obliged to go for work prevented his return every evening. At his own home, therefore, he saw Poverty in all its most affecting shapes, and when he speaks of it, as in the Address to Plenty, p. 48,

" Oh, sad sons of Poverty!
Victims doom'd to misery;
Who can paint what pain prevails
O'er that heart which want assails?
Modest Shame the pain conceals:
No one knows, but he who feels"——

And again :

> " Toiling in the naked fields,
> Where no bush a shelter yields,
> Needy Labour dithering stands,
> Beats and blows his numbing hands;
> And upon the crumping snows
> Stamps, in vain, to warm his toes"——

he utters " no idly-feign'd poetic pains:" it is a picture of what he has constantly witnessed and felt. One of our poets has gained great credit by his exterior delineations of what the poor man suffers; but in the reality of wretchedness, when " the iron enters into the soul," there is a tone which cannot be imitated. CLARE has here an unhappy advantage over other poets. The most miserable of them were not always wretched. Penury and disease were not constantly at their heels, nor was pauperism their only prospect. But he has no other, for the lot which has befallen his father, may, with too much reason, be looked forward to as his own portion. In the " simple annals of the poor" want occupies a part of every page, except, perhaps, the last, where the scene changes to the workhouse; and then the burthen which is taken from the body is laid upon the spirit: at least it would be so with CLARE; for though the contemplation of parochial relief may administer to some minds a thankless, hopeless sort of consolation, under the pressure of extreme distress, yet to the writer of the following lines it must be the highest aggravation of affliction :—

> " Oh, may I die, before I'm doom'd to seek
>   That last resource of hope, but ill supplied ;
> To claim the humble pittance once a week,
>   Which justice forces from disdainful pride!" (p. 78.)

While such was the destitute condition of his parents, it may seem extraordinary that CLARE should have found the means to acquire any learning whatever; but by extra work as a ploughboy, and by helping his father morning and evening at threshing, he earned the money which paid for his education. From the labour of eight weeks he generally acquired as many pence as would pay for a month's schooling; and thus in the course of three years he received, at different times, so much instruction that he could read very well in the Bible. He considers himself to have derived much benefit from the judicious encouragement of his schoolmaster, Mr. Seaton, of Glinton, an adjoining parish, from whom he sometimes obtained three-pence a week in rewards, and who once gave him sixpence for repeating, from memory, the third chapter of Job. With these little sums he bought a few books.

When he had learned to read tolerably well, he borrowed from one of his companions that universal favourite, Robinson Crusoe, and in the perusal of this he greatly increased his stock of knowledge and his desire for reading. He was thirteen years of age when another boy shewed him Thomson's Seasons. They were out in the fields together, and during the day CLARE had a good opportunity of looking at the book. It called forth all the passion of his soul for poetry. He was determined to possess the work himself; and as soon as he had saved a shilling to buy it with, he set off for Stamford at so early an hour, that none of the shops were open when he got there. It was a fine Spring morning, and when he had made his purchase, and was re-'turning through the beautiful scenery of Burghley Park, he composed his first piece of poetry, which he called " The Morning Walk." This was soon followed by the " Evening Walk," and some other little pieces.

But the first expression of his fondness for Poetry was before he had learnt to read. He was tired one day with looking at the pictures in a volume of poems, which he thinks were Pomfret's, when his father read him one piece in the book to amuse him. The delight he felt, at hearing this read, still warms him when he thinks of the circumstance ; but though he distinctly recollects the vivid pleasure which thrilled through him then, he has lost all trace of the incidents as well as of the language, nor can he find any poem of Pomfret's at all answering the faint conception he retains of it. It is possible that his chief gratification was in the harmony of the numbers, and that he had thoughts of his own floating onward with the verse very different from those which the same words would now suggest. The various melody of the earliest of his own compositions is some argument in favour of this opinion.

His love of Poetry, however, would soon have spent itself in compositions as little to be remembered as that which has just been mentioned, had it not been for the kindness of Mr. John Turnill, late of Helpstone, now in the Excise, who was indeed a benefactor to him. From his instruction CLARE, though he knew a little of the rudiments before, learnt Writing and Arithmetic; and to this friend he must, therefore, consider himself indebted for whatever good may accrue to him from the exercise of those powers of mind with which he is naturally endowed. For it is very probable, that, without the means of recording his productions on paper, CLARE would not only have lost the advantage he may derive from the publication of his works, but that also in himself he would not have been the

Poet he is; that, without writing down his thoughts, he could not have evolved them from his mind; and that his vocabulary would have been too scanty to express even what his imagination had strength enough to conceive. Besides, if he did succeed in partial instances, the aggregate amount of them could not have been collected and estimated. A few detached songs or short passages might be, perhaps, treasured in the memory of his companions for a short period, but they would soon perish. In his " Dawnings of Genius," CLARE describes the condition of a man, whose education has been too contracted to allow him to utter the thoughts of which he is conscious :—

> " Thus pausing wild on all he saunters by,
> He feels enraptur'd though he knows not why;
> And hums and mutters o'er his joys in vain,
> And dwells on something which he can't explain.
> The bursts of thought, with which his soul's perplex'd,
> Are bred one moment, and are gone the next;
> Yet still the heart will kindling sparks retain,
> And thoughts will rise, and Fancy strive again."

There is, perhaps, no feeling so distressing as this to the individual: it is an irremoveable nightmare, at it were, to Genius, which struggles in vain for sounds to convey an idea of its almost intolerable sensations,

" Till by successless sallies wearied quite,
The Memory fails, and Fancy takes her flight;
The wick confin'd within the socket dies,
Borne down and smother'd in a thousand sighs."

That this would have been CLARE's fate, unless he had been taught to write, cannot be doubted; and a perusal of his Poems will convince any one, that something of this kind he still feels, from his inability to find those words which can fully declare his meaning. From the want of a due supply of these, and from his ignorance of grammar, he seems to labour under great disadvantages. On the other hand, his want forces him to an extraordinary exertion of his native powers, in order to supply the deficiency. He employs the language under his command with great effect, in those unusual and unprecedented combinations of words which must be made, even by the learned, when they attempt to describe perfectly something which they have never seen or heard expressed before. And in this respect CLARE's deficiencies are the cause of many beauties,—for though he must, of course, innovate, that he may succeed in his purpose, yet he does it according to that rational mode of procedure, by which all languages have been formed and perfected. Thus he frequently makes verbs of substantives, as in the lines,

" Dark and darker *glooms* the sky"——

" To *pint* it just at my desire"——

Or of adjectives, as in the following,

" Spring's pencil *pinks* thee in thy flushy stain."

But in this he has done no more than the man who
first employed *crimson* as a verb : and as we had no
word that would in such brief compass supply so
clearly the sense of this, he was justified no doubt
in taking it. Some future writers may, perhaps,
feel thankful for the precedent. But there is no
innovation in such cases as these. Inseparably
connected with the use of speech is the privilege to
abbreviate; and those new ideas, which in one age
are obliged to be communicated paraphrastically,
have generally in the next some definite term as-
signed them : so legitimate, however, is the process
of this, by reason of certain laws of analogy which
are inherent in the mind of man, and universally
attended to in the formation of new words, that no
confusion can arise; for the word thus introduced
into a language always contains its meaning in its
derivation and composition, except it be such mere
cant as is not meant to live beyond the day; and
further, the correspondent word to it may always
be found in other more perfect languages, if the
people who spoke that language were alike conver-

sant with the idea, and equally under the tempta-
tion of employing some word to signify it.

But a very great number of those words which
are generally called new, are, in fact, some of the
oldest in our language : many of them are extant in
the works of our earliest authors ; and a still greater
number float on the popular voice, preserved only
by tradition, till the same things to which they were
originally applied again attract notice, and some
writer, in want of the word, either ignorantly or
wisely, but in either case happily, restores it to its
proper place.   Many of the provincial expressions,
to which CLARE has been forced to have recourse,
are of this description, forming part of a large num-
ber which may be called the unwritten language of
England.   They were once, perhaps, as current
throughout the land, and are still many of them as
well-sounding and significant, as any that are sanc-
tioned by the press.   In the midland counties they
are readily understood without a glossary; but, for
the use of those who are unaccustomed to them, all
such as are not to be found in Johnson's Dictionary
will be printed at the end, with explanations.

Another peculiarity in CLARE's writing, which
may be the occasion of some misunderstanding to
those who are critically nice in the construction of
a sentence, is the indifference with which he regards

words as governing each other; but this defect, which arises from his evident ignorance of grammar, is never so great as to give any real embarrassment to the reader*. An example occurs at p. 41 :—

" Just so 'twill fare with me in Autumn's Life,"

instead of for " the Autumn of Life;" but who can doubt the sense? And it may be worth while to mention here another line, which for the same reason may be objected to by some persons :—

" But still Hope's smiles unpoint the thorns of Care"——

as if he had intended to say " Hope smiling;" yet as the passage now stands it has also great propriety, and the Poet's conception of the effect of those smiles may have been, that they could blunt the thorns of care. But CLARE, as well as many other poets, does not regard language in the same way that a logician does. He considers it collectively rather than in detail, and paints up to his mind's original by mingling words, as a painter mixes his colours. And without this method, it would be impossible to convey to the understanding of the reader an adequate notion of some things, and

---

* The irregularity here mentioned was, from the same cause, practised by Shakspeare.—See Ritson's note, Shaks. vol. ii. p. 106. Edit. 21 vols. 1813.

especially of the effects of nature, seen under cer-
tain influences of time, circumstance, and colour.
In Prose these things are never attempted, unless
with great circumlocution; but Poetry is always
straining after them concisely, as they increase her
power of giving pleasure; and much allowance ought
to be made if her efforts in this way are not always
successful. Instances of the free grouping of words
occur in the Sonnet to the Glow-worm :—

" Tasteful Illumination of the night!
Bright, scatter'd, twinkling star of spangled earth," &c.

And in the following lines :—

" Aside the green hill's steepy brow,
Where shades the oak its darksome bough."
(p. 81.)

" So have I mark'd the dying embers light,——
With glimmering glow oft redden up again,
And sparks crack'd brightening into life, in vain."
(p. 149.)

" Brisk winds the lighten'd branches shake,
By pattering, plashing drops confess'd ;
And, where oaks dripping shade the lake,
Print crimpling dimples on its breast."
(p. 146.)

Examples of the use of Colour may be seen in
the Sonnets—To the Primrose, p. 188, The Gipsy's
Evening Blaze, p. 191, A Scene, p. 192, and in the
following verse :—

" First sunbeam, calling night away,
    To see how sweet thy summons seems,
Split by the willow's navy grey,
    And sweetly dancing on the streams."

(p. 142.)

The whole of the Sonnet to the river Gwash is an instance of it, down to the line

" And moss and ivy speckling on my eye."

A dry critic would call the former passages redundant in epithets; and the word *speckling* would excite, perhaps, his spleen in the latter: but ask the question, and you will probably find that this critic himself has no eye for colour,—that the light, and shade, and mezzotint of a landscape, have no charms for him,—that " his eye indeed is open, but its sense is shut;" and then, what dependance can be placed upon his judgment in these matters?

CLARE, it is evident, is susceptible of extreme pleasure from the varied hues, forms, and combinations in nature, and what he most enjoys, he endeavours to pourtray for the gratification of others. He is most thoroughly the Poet as well as the Child of Nature; and, according to his opportunities, no poet has more completely devoted himself to her service, studied her more closely, or exhibited so many sketches of her under new and interesting appearances. There is some merit in all this, for

Wordsworth asserts, "that, excepting a passage or two in the Windsor Forest of Pope, and some delightful pictures in the Poems of Lady Winchelsea, the Poetry of the period intervening between the publication of the Paradise Lost, and the Seasons [60 years], does not contain a single new image of external nature." But CLARE has no idea of excelling others in doing this. He loves the fields, the flowers, " the common air, the sun, the skies;" and, therefore, he writes about them. He is happier in the presence of Nature than elsewhere. He looks as anxiously on her face as if she were a living friend, whom he might lose; and hence he has learnt to notice every change in her countenance, and to delineate all the delicate varieties of her character. Most of his poems were composed under the immediate impression of this feeling, in the fields, or on the road-sides. He could not trust his memory, and therefore he wrote them down with a pencil on the spot, his hat serving him for a desk; and if it happened that he had no opportunity soon after of transcribing these imperfect memorials, he could seldom decypher them, or recover his first thoughts. From this circumstance several of his poems are quite lost, and others exist only in fragments. Of those which he had committed to writing, especially his earlier pieces, many were destroyed from another circumstance, which shews how little he expected to please others with them : from a hole in the wall of his room, where he stuffed his manuscripts, a piece of paper was often taken to hold the kettle, or light the fire.

It is now thirteen years since CLARE composed his first poem: in all that time he has gone on secretly cultivating his taste and talent for poetry, without one word of encouragement, or the most distant prospect of reward. That passion must have been originally very strong and pure, which could sustain itself, for so many years, through want, and toil, and hopeless misery. His labour in the fields through all seasons, it might be thought, would have disgusted him with those objects which he so much admired at first; and his taste might have altered with his age: but the foundation of his regard was laid too deeply in truth to be shaken. On the contrary, he found delight in scenes which no other poet has thought of celebrating. "The swampy falls of pasture ground, and rushy spreading greens," "plashy streams," and "weed-beds wild and rank," give him as much real transport as common minds feel at what are called the most romantic prospects. And if there were any question as to the intensity or sincerity of his feeling for Poetry and Nature, the commendation of these simple, unthought of, and generally despised objects would decide it.

Of the poems which form the present collection some few were among CLARE's earliest efforts. The Fate of Amy was begun when he was fourteen; Helpstone, The Gipsy's Evening Blaze, Reflection in Autumn, The Robin, Noon, The Universal Epitaph, and some others, were written before he was seventeen. The rest bear various dates, but the greater number are of recent origin. The Village Funeral was written in 1815; The Address to Plenty, in December 1817; The Elegy on the Ruins of Pickworth, in 1818. To describe the occupations of CLARE, we must not say that Labour and the Muse went hand in hand: they rather kept alternate watch, and when Labour was exhausted with fatigue, she " cheer'd his needy toilings with a song." In a note on this poem, CLARE says, " The Elegy on the Ruins of Pickworth was written one Sunday morning, after I had been helping to dig the hole for a lime-kiln, where the many fragments of mortality and perished ruins inspired me with thoughts of other times, and warmed me into song."

In the last two years he has written, What is Life? The Fountain, My Mary, To a Rosebud, Effusion to Poesy, The Summer Evening, Summer Morning, First of May, The Dawnings of

Genius, The Contrast, Dolly's Mistake, Harvest
Morning, The Poet's Wish, Crazy Nell, and
several other pieces, with almost all the Sonnets.
One of the last productions of CLARE's fancy is the
following Song, which, as it came too late to be in-
serted in its proper place in this volume, may as
well appear here, where it fitly closes the chronicle
of his Poems.

THE MEETING.

HERE we meet, too soon to part,
Here to leave will raise a smart,
Here I'll press thee to my heart,
    Where none have place above thee
Here I vow to love thee well,
And could words unseal the spell,
Had but language strength to tell,
    I'd say how much I love thee.

Here, the rose that decks thy door,
Here, the thorn that spreads thy bow'r,
Here, the willow on the moor,
    The birds at rest above thee,
Had they light of life to see,
Sense of soul like thee and me
Soon might each a witness be
    How doatingly I love thee.

By the night-sky's purple ether,
And by even's sweetest weather,
That oft has blest us both together,—
    The moon that shines above thee,
And shews thy beauteous cheek so blooming,
And by pale age's winter coming,
The charms, and casualties of woman,
    I will for ever love thee.

This song is written nearly in the metre of one by Burns, " O were I on Parnassus' Hill," and the subject is the same, but in the execution they are quite different. CLARE has a great delight in trying to run races with other men, and unluckily this cannot always be attempted without subjecting him to the charge of imitating ; but he will be found free from this imputation in all the best parts of his poetry, and in the present instance it may be worth while comparing him with his prototype, to see how little he stands in need of such assistance. The propensity to emulate another is a youthful emotion, and in his friendless state it afforded him an obvious, and, perhaps, the only mode of endeavouring to ascertain what kind and degree of ability he possessed as a Poet.

This song, " The Meeting," was written at Helpstone, where CLARE is again residing with his parents, working for any one who will employ him, but without any regular occupation. He had an engagement during the greater part of the year with Mr. Wilders, of Bridge-Casterton, two miles north of Stamford; where the river Gwash, which crosses the road, gave him a subject for one of his Sonnets. (p. 203.) His wages were nine shillings a week, and his food; out of which he had to pay one shilling and sixpence a week for a bed, it being impossible that he could return every night to Helpstone, a distance of nine miles: but at the beginning of November, his employer proposed to allow him only seven shillings a week, on which he quitted his service and returned home.

It was an accident which led to the publication of these Poems. In December 1818, Mr. Edward Drury, Bookseller, of Stamford, met by chance with the Sonnet to the Setting Sun, written on a piece of paper in which a letter had been wrapped up, and signed J. C. Having ascertained the name and residence of the writer, he went to Helpstone, where he saw some other poems with which he was much pleased. At his request, CLARE made a collection of the pieces he had written, and added some others to them. They were then sent to London, and the publishers selected those which form the present volume. They have been printed with the usual corrections only of orthography and grammar, in such instances as allowed of its being done without changing the words: the proofs were then revised by CLARE, and a few alterations were made at his desire. The original MSS. may be seen at Messrs. Taylor and Hessey's.

The Author and his Poems are now before the public; and its decision will speedily fix the fate of the one, and, ultimately, that of the other: but whatever be the result to either, this will at least be granted, that no Poet of our country has shewn greater ability, under circumstances so hostile to its developement. And all this is found here without any of those distressing and revolting alloys, which too often debase the native worth of genius, and make him who was gifted with powers to command admiration, live to be the object of contempt or pity. The lower the condition of its possessor, the more unfavourable, generally, has been the effect of genius on his life. That this has not been the case with CLARE may, perhaps, be imputed to the abso-lute depression of his fortune. It is certain that he bas not had the opportunity hitherto of being injured by prosperity; and that he may escape in future, it is hoped that those persons who intend to shew him kindness, will not do it suddenly or partially, but so as it will yield him permanent benefit. Yet when we hear the consciousness of possessing talent, and the natural irritability of the poetic temperament, pleaded in extenuation of the follies and vices of men in high life, let it be accounted no mean praise to such a man as CLARE, that, with all the excitements of *their* sensibility in *his* station, he has preserved a fair character, amid dangers which presumption did not create, and difficulties which discretion could not avoid. In the real troubles of life, when they are not brought on by the misconduct of the individual, a strong mind acquires the power of righting itself after each attack, and this philosophy, not to call it by a better name, CLARE possesses. If the expectations of " better life," which he cannot help indulging, should all be disappointed, by the coldness with which this volume may be received, he can

" —— put up with distress, and be content."

(p. 4)

In one of his letters he says, " If my hopes don't succeed, the hazard is not of much cousequence : if I fall, I am advanced at no great distance from my low condition : if I sink for want of friends, my old friend Necessity is ready to help me, as before. It was never my fortune as yet to meet advancement from friendship : my fate has ever been hard labour among the most vulgar and

lowest conditions of men; and very small is the
pittance hard labour allows n\e, though I always
toil'd even beyond my strength to obtain it."—To
see a man of talent struggling under great adversity
with such a spirit, must surely excite in every gene-
rous heart the wish to befriend him.   But if it be
otherwise, and he should be doomed to remediless
misery,

> " Why let the stricken deer go weep,
>   The hart ungalled play;
> For some must watch, while some must sleep,—
>   Thus runs the world away."

CONTENTS.

POEMS.

SONGS AND BALLADS.

––––

SONNETS.

POEMS.

POEMS.

HELPSTONE.

HAIL, humble Helpstone! where thy vallies spread,

And thy mean village lifts its lowly head;

Unknown to grandeur, and unknown to fame;

No minstrel boasting to advance thy name ·

Unletter'd spot! unheard in poets' song;

Where bustling labour drives the hours along;

Where dawning genius never met the day;

Where useless ignorance slumbers life away;

Unknown nor heeded, where, low genius tries

Above the vulgar and the vain to rise.

Mysterious Fate! who can on thee depend?
Thou opes the hour, but hides its doubtful end:
In Fancy's view the joys have long appear'd,
Where the glad heart by laughing plenty's cheer'd;
And Fancy's eyes as oft, as vainly, fill;
At first but doubtful, and as doubtful still.
So little birds, in winter's frost and snow,
Doom'd, like to me, want's keener frost to know;
Searching for food and " better life," in vain,
Each hopeful track the yielding snows retain;
First on the ground each fairy dream pursue,
Though sought in vain; yet bent on higher view,
Still chirp, and hope, and wipe each glossy bill;
And undiscourag'd, undishearten'd still,
Hop on the snow-cloth'd bough, and chirp again,
Heedless of naked shade and frozen plain:
Till, like to me, these victims of the blast,
Each foolish, fruitless wish resign'd at last,
Are glad to seek the place from whence they went
And put up with distress, and be content.

Hail, scenes obscure! so near and dear to me,
The church, the brook, the cottage, and the tree ˙
Still shall obscurity rehearse the song,
And hum your beauties as I stroll along.
Dear, native spot! which length of time endears;
The sweet retreat of twenty lingering years,
And, oh! those years of infancy the scene;
Those dear delights, where once they all have been;
Those golden days, long vanish'd from the plain;
Those sports, those pastimes, now belov'd in vain;
When happy youths in pleasure's circle ran,
Nor thought what pains awaited future man;
No other thought employing, or employ'd,
But how to add to happiness enjoy'd:
Each morning wak'd with hopes before unknown,
And eve, possessing, made each wish their own;
The day gone by left no pursuit undone,
Nor one vain wish, save that it went too soon;
Each sport, each pastime, ready at their call,
As soon as wanted they possess'd them all:

These joys, all known in happy infancy,

And all I ever knew, were spent in thee.

And who, but loves to view where these were past?

And who that views, but loves them to the last?

Feels his heart warm to view his native place,

A fondness still those past delights to trace?

The vanish'd green to mourn, the spot to see

Where flourish'd many a bush and many a tree?

Where once the brook, for now the brook is gone,

O'er pebbles dimpling sweet went whimpering on;

Oft on whose oaken plank I've wondering stood,

(That led a pathway o'er its gentle flood),

To see the beetles their wild mazes run,

With jetty jackets glittering in the sun:

So apt and ready at their reels they seem,

So true the dance is figur'd on the stream,

Such justness, such correctness they impart,

They seem as ready as if taught by art.

In those past days, for then I lov'd the shade,

How oft I've sigh'd at alterations made;

To see the woodman's cruel axe employ'd,

A tree beheaded, or a bush destroy'd:

Nay e'en a post, old standard, or a stone

Moss'd o'er by age, and branded as her own,

Would in my mind a strong attachment gain,

A fond desire that there they might remain;

And all old favourites, fond taste approves,

Griev'd me at heart to witness their removes.

Thou far fled pasture, long evanish'd scene !

Where nature's freedom spread the flow'ry green;

Where golden kingcups open'd into view;

Where silver daisies in profusion grew;

And, tottering, hid amidst those brighter gems,

Where silken grasses bent their tiny stems;

Where the pale lilac, mean and lowly, grew,

Courting in vain each gazer's heedless view;

While cowslips, sweetest flowers upon the plain,

Seemingly how'd to shun the hand, in vain:

Where lowing oxen roam'd to feed at large,
And bleating there the shepherd's woolly charge,
Whose constant calls thy echoing vallies cheer'd,
Thy scenes adorn'd, and rural life endear'd;
No calls of hunger pity's feelings wound,
'Twas wanton plenty rais'd the joyful sound:
Thy grass in plenty gave the wish'd supply,
Ere sultry suns had wak'd the troubling fly;
Then blest retiring, by thy bounty fed,
They sought thy shades, and found an easy bed.

But now, alas! those scenes exist no more;
The pride of life with thee, like mine, is o'er,
Thy pleasing spots to which fond memory clings,
Sweet cooling shades, and soft refreshing springs.
And though fate's pleas'd to lay their beauties by
In a dark corner of obscurity,
As fair and sweet they bloom'd thy plains among,
As bloom those Edens by the poets sung;

Now all laid waste by desolation's hand,
Whose cursed weapon levels half the land.
Oh! who could see my dear green willows fall,
What feeling heart, but dropt a tear for all? -
Accursed Wealth! o'er-bounding human laws,
Of every evil thou remain'st the cause.
Victims of want, those wretches such as me,
Too truly lay their wretchedness to thee :
Thou art the bar that keeps from being fed,
And thine our loss of labour and of bread;
Thou art the cause that levels every tree,
And woods bow down to clear a way for thee.

Sweet rest and peace! ye dear, departed charms,
Which industry once cherish'd in her arms;
When ease and plenty, known but now to few,
Were known to all, and labour had its due;
When mirth and toil, companions through the day,
Made labour light, and pass'd the hours away;

When nature made the fields so dear to me,

Thin scattering many a bush and many a tree;

Where the wood minstrel sweetly join'd among,

And cheer'd my needy toilings with a song;

Ye perish'd spots, adieu! ye ruin'd scenes,

Ye well known pastures, oft frequented greens!

Though now no more, fond Memory's pleasing pains,

Within her breast your every scene retains.

Scarce did a bush spread its romantic bower,

To shield the lazy shepherd from the shower;

Scarce did a tree befriend the chattering pye,

By lifting up its head so proud and high;

No, not a secret spot did then remain,

Throughout each spreading wood and winding plain,

But, in those days, my presence once possess'd,

The snail-horn searching, or the mossy nest.

Oh, happy Eden of those golden years

Which memory cherishes, and use endears,

Thou dear, beloved spot! may it be thine

To add a comfort to my life's decline,

When this vain world and I have nearly done,

And Time's drain'd glass has little left to run.

When all the hopes, that charm'd me once, are o'er,

To warm my soul in extacy no more,

By disappointments prov'd a foolish cheat,

Each ending bitter, and beginning sweet;

When weary age the grave, a rescue, seeks,

And prints its image on my wrinkled cheeks,—

Those charms of youth, that I again may see,

May it be mine to meet my end in thee;

And, as reward for all my troubles past,

Find one hope true—to die at home at last!

ADDRESS TO A LARK,

SINGING IN WINTER.

Ay, little Larky! what's the reason,
Singing thus in winter season?
Nothing, surely, can be pleasing
    To make thee sing;
For I see nought but cold and freezing,
    And feel its sting.

Perhaps, all done with silent mourning,
Thou think'st that summer is returning,
And this the last, cold, frosty morning,
    To chill thy breast;
If so, I pity thy discerning:
    And so I've guess'd.

Poor, little Songster! vainly cheated;
Stay, leave thy singing uncompleted;
Drop where,thou wast beforehand seated,
    In thy warm nest;
Nor let vain wishes be repeated,
    But sit at rest.

'Tis winter; let the cold content thee:
Wish after nothing till its sent thee,
For disappointments will torment thee,
    Which will be thine:
I know it well, for I've had plenty
    Misfortunes mine.

Advice, sweet Warbler! don't despise it:
None know what's what, but he that tries it;
And then he well knows how to prize it,
    And so do I:
Thy ease, with mine I sympathise it,
    With many a sigh.

Vain Hope! of thee I've had my portion;
Mere flimsy cobweb! changing ocean!
That flits the scene at every motion,
  And still eggs on,
With sweeter view, and stronger notion
  To dwell upon:

Yes, I've dwelt long on idle fancies,
Strange and uncommon as romances,
On future luck my noddle dances,
  What I would be;
But, ah! when future time advances,
  All's blank to me.

Now twenty years I've pack'd behind me,
Since hope's deluding tongue inclin'd me
To fuss myself. But, Warbler, mind me,
  It's all a sham;
And twenty more's as like to find me
  Just as I am.

I'm poor enough, there's plenty knows it;
Obscure; how dull, my scribbling shows it:
Then sure 'twas madness to suppose it,
　　What I was at,
To gain preferment! there I'll close it:
　　So mum for that.

Let mine, sweet Bird then be a warning:
Advice in season don't be scorning,
But wait till Spring's first days are dawning
　　To glad and cheer thee;
And then, sweet Minstrel of the morning,
　　I'd wish to hear thee.

THE FATE OF AMY.

A TALE.

BENEATH a sheltering wood's warm side,
    Where many a tree expands
Its branches o'er the neighbouring brook,
    A ruin'd cottage stands ·

Though now left desolate, and lost
    Its origin, and all;
Owls hooting from the roofless walls,
    Rejoicing in its fall;

A time was once, remembrance knows,
    Though now the time's gone by,
When that was seen to flourish gay,
    And pleasing to the eye.

On that same ground the brambles hide,
    And stinking weeds o'errun,
An orchard bent its golden boughs,
    And redden'd in the sun.

Yon nettles where they're left to spread,
    There once a garden smil'd;
And lovely was the spot to view,
    Though now so lost and wild:

And where the sickly alder loves
    To top the mouldering wall;
And ivy's kind encroaching care
    Delays the tottering fall;

There once a mother's only joy,
    A daughter lovely, fair,
As ever bloom'd beneath the sun,
    Was nurs'd and cherish'd there.

The cottage then was known around;
  The neighbouring village swains
Would often wander by to view
  That charmer of the plains.

Where softest blush of roses wild,
  And hawthorn's fairest blow,
But meanly serve to paint her cheek,
  And bosom's rival snow;

The loveliest blossom of the plains,
  The artless Amy prov'd;
In nature's sweetest charms adorn'd,
  Those charms by all belov'd.

Sweet Innocence! the beauty's thine
  That every bosom warms.
Fair as she was, she liv'd alone
  A stranger to her charms.

Unmov'd the praise of swains she heard,
  Nor proud at their despair;
But thought they scoff'd her when they prais'd;
  And knew not she was fair.

Nor did she for the joys of youth
  Forsake her mother's side,
Who then by age and pain infirm'd,
  On her for help relied.

No tenderer mother to a child
  Throughout the world could be;
And, in return, no daughter prov'd
  More dutiful than she.

The pains of age she sympathiz'd
  And sooth'd, and wish'd to share
In short, the aged, helpless dame
  Was Amy's only care.

But age had pains, and they were all:
    Life's cares they little knew;
Its billows ne'er encompass'd them,
    They waded smoothly through.

The tender father, now no more,
    Did for them both provide;
The wealth his industry had gain'd,
    All wants to come supplied.

Kind heaven upon their labours smil'd;
    Industry gave increase;
The cottage was contentment's own
    Abode of health and peace.

Alas! the tongue of Fate is seal'd,
    And kept for ever dumb:
To-morrow's met with blinded eyes;
    We know not what's to come.

Blithe as the lark, as cricket gay
  That chirrup'd on the hearth,
This Sun of Beauty's time was spent
  In inoffensive mirth.

Meek as the lambs that throng'd her door,
  As innocent as they,
Her hours pass'd on, and charms improv'd
  With each succeeding day.

So, smiling on the sunny plain,
  The lovely daisies blow,
Unconscious of the careless foot
  That lays their beauty low.

So blooms the lily of the vale;
  (Ye beauties, oh, be wise!)
Untimely blasts o'ertake its bloom,
  It withers, and it dies.

The humble cottage lonely stood
   Far from the neighbouring vill;
Its church, that topp'd the willow groves,
   Lay far upon the hill:

Which made all company desir'd,
   And welcome to the dame;
And oft to tell the village news,
   The neighbouring gossips came.

Young Edward mingled with the rest:
   An artful swain was he,
Who laugh'd, and told his merry jests;
   For custom made him free:

And oft with Amy toy'd and play'd,
   While, harmless as the dove,
Her artless, unsuspecting heart
   But little thought of love.

But frequent visits gain'd esteem,
    Each time of longer stay;
And custom did his name endear :—
    He stole her heart away.'

So fairest flowers adorn the wild ;
    And most endanger'd stand
The soonest seen,—a certain prey
    To some destroying hand.

Her choice was fix'd on him alone ;
    The rest but vainly strove :
And worse than all the rest is he ;
    But blind the eyes of love.

Of him full many a maid complain'd,
    The lover of an hour,
That like the ever changing bee,
    Sipp'd sweets from every flower.

Alas! those slighted pains are small,
   If all such maidens know;
But she was fair, and he design'd
   To work her further woe.

Her innocence his bosom fir'd,
   So long'd to be enjoy'd;
And he, to gain his wish'd-for ends,
   Each subtle art employ'd.

Ah! he employed his subtle arts,
   Alas, too sad to tell;
The winning ways which he employed,
   Succeeded but too well.

So artless, innocent, and young,
   So ready to believe;
A stranger to the world was she,
   And easy to deceive.

Ah! now farewel to beauty's boast,
  Charms so admir'd before;
Now innocence has lost its sweets,
  Her beauties bloom no more.

The flowers the sultry summer kills,
  Spring's milder suns restore;
But innocence, that fickle charm,
  Blooms once, and blooms no more.

The swains who lov'd, no more admire,
  Their hearts no beauty warms;
And maidens triumph in her fall,
  That envied once her charms.

Lost was that sweet simplicity;
  Her eye's bright lustre fled;
And o'er her cheeks, where roses bloom'd,
  A sickly paleness spread.

So fades the flower before its time,

    Where canker-worms assail;

So droops the bud upon its stem,

    Beneath the sickly gale.

The mother saw the sudden change,

    Where health so lately smil'd;

Too much—and, oh! suspecting more,

    Grew anxious for her child.

And all the kindness in her power,

    The tender mother shows;

In hopes such kindly means would make

    Her fearless to disclose.

And oft she hinted, if a crime,

    Through ignorance beguil'd—

Not to conceal the crime in fear,

    For none should wrong her child:

Or, if the rose that left her cheek
    Was banish'd by disease,
" Fear God, my child ! " she oft would say,
    " And you may hope for ease."

And still she pray'd, and still had hopes
    There was no injury done;
And still advis'd the ruin'd girl,
    The world's deceit to shun.

And many a cautionary tale
    Of hapless maiden's fate,
From trusting man, to warn her, told;
    But told, alas ! too late.

A tender mother's painful cares,
    In vain the loss supply;
The wide-mouth'd world, its sport and scorn
    Than meet, she'd sooner die.

Advice but aggravated woe;

    And ease, an empty sound;

No one could ease the pains she felt,

    But he who gave the wound.

And he, wild youth, had left her now,

    Unfeeling as the stone:

Fair maids, beware, lest careless ways

    Make Amy's fate your own.

Ill-fated girl! too late she found,

    As but too many find,

False Edward's love as light as down,

    And vows as fleet as wind.

But one hope's left, and that she sought,

    To hide approaching shame;

And Pity, while she drops a tear,

    Forbears the rest to name.

The widow'd mother, though so old,
   And ready to depart,
Was not ordain'd to live her time;
   The sad news broke her heart.

Borne down beneath a weight of years,
   And all the pains they gave,
But little added weight requir'd
   To crush her in the grave.

The strong oak braves the rudest wind;
   While, to the breeze, as well
The sickly, aged willow falls,—
   And so the mother fell.

Beside the pool the willow bends,
   The dew-bent daisy weeps;
And where the turfy hillock swells,
   The luckless Amy sleeps.

EVENING.

Now grey-ey'd hazy Eve's begun
    To shed her balmy dew,
Insects no longer fear the sun,
    But come in open view.

Now buzzing, with unwelcome din,
    The heedless beetle bangs
Against the cow-boy's dinner tin,
    That o'er his shoulder hangs.

And on he keeps in heedless pat,
    Till, quite enrag'd, the boy
Pulls off his weather-beaten hat,
    Resolving to destroy.

Yet thoughtless that he wrong'd the clown,
  By blows he'll not be driven,
But buzzes on, till batter'd down
  For unmeant injury given.

Now from each hedge-row fearless peep
  The slowly-pacing snails,
Betraying their meand'ring creep,
  In silver-slimy trails.

The dew-worms too in couples start,
  But leave their holes in fear;
For in a moment they will part,
  If aught approaches near.

The owls mope out, and scouting bats
  Begin their giddy round;
While countless swarms of dancing gnats
  Each water-pudge surround.

And 'side yon pool, as smooth as glass,
  Reflecting every cloud,
Securely hid among the grass,
  The crickets chirrup loud.

That rural call, " *Come mulls! come mulls!*"
  From distant pasture grounds,
All noises now to silence lulls,
  In soft and ushering sounds;

While echoes weak, from hill to hill
  Their dying sounds deplore,
That whimper faint and fainter still,
  Till they are heard no more.

The breezes, once so cool and brief,
  At Eve's approach all died;
None's left to make the aspen leaf
  Twirl up its hoary side.

But breezes all are useless now;
   The hazy dun, that spreads
Her moist'ning dew on every bough,
   Sufficient coolness sheds.

The flowers, reviving from the ground,
   Perk up again and peep,
While many different tribes around
   Are shutting up to sleep.

Now let me, hid in cultur'd plain,
   Pursue my evening walk,
Where each way beats the nodding grain,
   Aside the narrow baulk;

While fairy visions intervene,
   Creating dread surprize,
From distant objects dimly seen,
   That catch the doubtful eyes.

And fairies now, no doubt, unseen,
    In silent revels sup;
With dew-drop bumpers toast their queen,
    From crow-flower's golden cup.

Although about these tiny things
    Folks make so much ado;
I never heed the darksome rings,
    Where they are said to go :

But superstition still deceives;
    And fairies still prevail;
While stooping genius e'en believes
    The customary tale.

Oh, loveliest time! oh, sweetest hours
    The musing soul can find!
Now, Evening, let thy soothing powers
    At freedom fill the mind.

WHAT IS LIFE?

———

AND what is Life?—An hour-glass on the run,

A mist retreating from the morning sun,

  A busy, bustling, still repeated dream;

Its length?—A minute's pause, a moment's thought;

  And happiness?—A bubble on the stream,

That in the act of seizing shrinks to nought.

What are vain Hopes?—The puffing gale of morn,

  That of its charms divests the dewy lawn,

And robs each flow'ret of its gem,—and dies;

  A cobweb hiding disappointment's thorn,

Which stings more keenly through the thin disguise.

And thou, O Trouble?—nothing can suppose,

(And sure the power of wisdom only knows,)

    What need requireth thee:

So free and liberal as thy bounty flows,

    Some necessary cause must surely be:

But disappointments, pains, and every woe

    Devoted wretches feel,

The universal plagues of life below,

    Are mysteries still 'neath Fate's unbroken seal.

And what is Death? is still the cause unfound?

That dark, mysterious name of horrid sound?—

    A long and lingering sleep, the weary crave.

And Peace? where can its happiness abound?—

    No where at all, save heaven, and the grave.

Then what is Life?—When stripp'd of its disguise,

    A thing to be desir'd it cannot be;

Since every thing that meets our foolish eyes

Gives proof sufficient of its vanity.

'Tis but a trial all must undergo;

To teach unthankful mortals how to prize

That happiness vain man's denied to know,

Until he's call'd to claim it in the skies.

ON A LOST GREYHOUND

LYING ON THE SNOW.

AH, thou poor, neglected hound!

Now thou'st done with catching hares,

Thou mayst lie upon the ground,

Lost, for what thy master cares.

To see thee lie, it makes me sigh :
   A proud, hard hearted man !
But men, we know, like dogs may go,
   When they've done all they can.

And thus, from witnessing thy fate,
   Thoughtful reflection wakes;
Though thou'rt a dog, with grief I say't,
   Poor man thy fare partakes :
Like thee, lost whelp, the poor man's help,
   Erewhile so much desir'd,
Now harvest's got, is wanted not,
   Or little is requir'd.

So now, the overplus will be
   As useless negroes, all
Turn'd in the bitter blast, like thee
   Mere cumber-grounds, to fall :

But this reward, for toil so hard,
   Is sure to meet return
From Him, whose ear is always near,
   When the oppressed mourn.

For dogs, as men, are equally
   A link of Nature's chain,
Form'd by that hand that formed me,
   Which formeth nought in vain.
All life contains, as 'twere by chains,
   From Him still perfect are;
Nor does He think the meanest link
   Unworthy of His care.

So let us both on Him rely,
   And He'll for us provide;
Find us a shelter warm and dry,
   And every thing beside.

And while fools, void of sense, deride

   My tenderness to thee;

I'll take thee home, from whence I've come:

   So rise, and gang with me.

Poor, patient thing! he seems to hear

   And know what I have said;

He wags his tail, and ventures near,

   And bows his mournful head.

Thou'rt welcome: come! and though thou'rt dumb,

   Thy silence speaks thy pains;

So with me start, to share a part,

   While I have aught remains.

A REFLECTION IN AUTUMN.

Now Autumn's come, adieu the pleasing greens,
   The charming landscape, and the flow'ry plain!
All have deserted from these motley scenes,
   With blighted yellow ting'd, and russet stain.

Though desolation seems to triumph here,
   Yet this is Spring to what we still shall find
The trees must all in nakedness appear,
   'Reft of their foliage by the blustry wind.

Just so 'twill fare with me in Autumn's Life;
   Just so I'd wish: but may the trunk and all
Die with the leaves; nor taste that wintry strife,
   When sorrows urge, and fear impedes the fall.

THE ROBIN.

Now the snow hides the ground, little birds leave
    the wood,
And fly to the cottage to beg for their food;
While the Robin, domestic, more tame than the rest,
With its wings drooping down, and its feathers
    undrest,
Comes close to our windows, as much as to say,
" I would venture in, if I could find a way:
I'm starv'd, and I want to get out of the cold;
Oh! make me a passage, and think me not bold."
Ah, poor little creature! thy visits reveal
Complaints such as these, to the heart that can feel:
Nor shall such complainings be urged in vain;
I'll make thee a hole, if I take out a pane.

Come in, and a welcome reception thou'lt find :

I keep no grimalkin to murder inclin'd.

But oh, little Robin ! be careful to shun

That house, where the peasant makes use of a gun ;

For if thou but taste of the seed he has strew'd,

Thy life as a ransom must pay for the food :

His aim is unerring, his heart is as hard ;

And thy race, though so harmless, he'll never regard.

Distinction with him, boy, is nothing at all ;

Both the Wren, and the Robin, with Sparrows must

      fall.

For his soul (though he outwardly looks like a man,)

Is in nature a wolf of the Apennine clan ;

Like them his whole study is bent on his prey :

Then be careful, and shun what is meant to betray.

Come, come to my cottage ; and thou shalt be free

To perch on my finger, and sit on my knee :

Thou shalt eat of the crumbles of bread to thy fill,

And have leisure to clean both thy feathers and bill.

Then come, little Robin! and never believe

Such warm invitations are meant to deceive:

In duty I'm bound to show mercy on thee,

Since God don't deny it to sinners like me.

———◆———

EPIGRAM.

———

FOR fools that would wish to seem learned and
     wise,

   This receipt a wise man did bequeath :—

" Let 'em have the free use of their ears and their
     eyes;

   " But their tongue," says he, " tie to their teeth."

ADDRESS TO PLENTY,

IN WINTER.

O THOU Bliss! to riches known,

Stranger to the poor alone;

Giving most where none's requir'd,

Leaving none where most's desir'd;

Who, sworn friend to miser, keeps

Adding to his useless heaps

Gifts on gifts profusely stor'd,

Till thousands swell the mouldy hoard:

While poor, shatter'd Poverty,

To advantage seen in me,

With his rags, his wants, and pain,

Waking pity but in vain,

Bowing, cringing at thy side,

Begs his mite, and is denied.

O, thou Blessing! let not me
Tell as vain my wants to thee;
Thou, by name of Plenty stil'd,
Fortune's heir, her favourite child.
'Tis a maxim—hunger feed,
Give the needy when they need;
He, whom all profess to serve,
The same maxim did observe ·
Their obedience here, how well,
Modern times will plainly tell.
Hear my wants, nor deem me bold,
Not without occasion told:
Hear one wish; nor fail to give;
Use me well, and bid me live.

'Tis not great, what I solicit;
Was it more, thou couldst not miss it:
Now the cutting winter's come,
'Tis but just to find a home,
In some shelter, dry and warm,
That will shield me from the storm.

Toiling in the naked fields,

Where no bush a shelter yields,

Needy Labour dithering stands,

Beats and blows his numbing hands;

And upon the crumping snows

Stamps, in vain, to warm his toes.

Leaves are fled, that once had power

To resist a summer shower;

And the wind so piercing blows,

Winnowing small the drifting snows,

The summer shade of loaded bough

Would vainly boast a shelter now ·

Piercing snows so searching fall,

They sift a passage through them all.

Though all's vain to keep him warm,

Poverty must brave the storm.

Friendship none, its aid to lend :

Health alone his only friend;

Granting leave to live in pain,

Giving strength to toil in vain;

To be, while winter's horrors last,
The sport of every pelting blast.

Oh, sad sons of Poverty!
Victims doom'd to misery;
Who can paint what pain prevails
O'er that heart which want assails?
Modest Shame the pain conceals:
No one knows, but he who feels.
Oh, thou charm which Plenty crowns,
Fortune! smile, now Winter frowns:
Cast around a pitying eye;
Feed the hungry ere they die.
Think, oh! think upon the poor,
Nor against them shut thy door ·
Freely let thy bounty flow,
On the sons of want and woe.

Hills and dales no more are seen,
In their dress of pleasing green;

Summer's robes are all thrown by,

For the clothing of the sky;

Snows on snows in heaps combine,

Hillocks, rais'd as mountains, shine,

And at distance rising proud,

Each appears a fleecy cloud.

Plenty, now thy gifts bestow;

Exit bid to every woe:

Take me in, shut out the blast,

Make the doors and windows fast;

Place me in some corner, where,

Lolling in an elbow chair,

Happy, blest to my desire,

I may find a rouzing fire;

While in chimney-corner nigh,

Coal, or wood, a fresh supply,

Ready stands for laying on,

Soon as t'other's burnt and gone.

Now and then, as taste decreed,

In a book a page I'd read;

And inquiry to amuse,

Peep at something in the news;

See who's married, and who's dead,

And who, through bankrupt, beg their bread:

While on hob, or table nigh,

Just to drink before I'm dry,

A pitcher at my side should stand

With the barrel nigh at hand,

Always ready as I will'd,

When 'twas empty, to be fill'd;

And, to be possess'd of all,

A corner cupboard in the wall,

With store of victuals lin'd complete,

That when hungry I might eat.

Then would I in Plenty's lap,

For the first time take a nap;

Falling back in easy lair,

Sweetly slumb'ring in my chair;

With no reflective thoughts to wake

Pains that cause my heart to ache,

Of contracted debts long made,

In no prospect to be paid;

And, to want, sad news severe,

Of provisions getting dear:

While the winter, shocking sight,

Constant freezes day and night,

Deep and deeper falls the snow,

Labour's slack, and wages low.

These, and more, the poor can tell,

Known, alas! by them too well,

Plenty! oh, if blest by thee,

Never more should trouble me.

Hours and weeks will sweetly glide,

Soft and smooth as flows the tide,

Where no stones or choaking grass

Force a curve ere it can pass:

And as happy, and as blest,

As beasts drop them down to rest,

When in pastures at their will,

They have roam'd and eat their fill;

Soft as nights in summer creep,

So should I then fall asleep;

While sweet visions of delight,

So enchanting to the sight,

Sweetly swimming o'er my eyes,

Would sink me into extacies.

Nor would Pleasure's dreams once more,

As they oft have done before,

Cause be to create a pain,

When I woke to find them vain

Bitter past, the present sweet,

Would my happiness complete.

Oh! how easy I should lie,

With the fire up-blazing high,

(Summer's artificial bloom,)

That like an oven keeps the room,

Or lovely May, as mild and warm:

While, without, the raging storm

Is roaring in the chimney-top,

In no likelihood to drop;

And the witchen-branches nigh,

O'er my snug box towering high,

That sweet shelter'd stands beneath,

In convulsive eddies wreathe.

Then while, tyrant-like, the storm

Takes delight in doing harm,

Down before him crushing all,

Till his weapons useless fall;

And as in oppression proud,

Peal his howlings long and loud,

While the clouds, with horrid sweep,

Give (as suits a tyrant's trade)

The sun a minute's leave to peep,

To smile upon the ruins made;

And to make complete the blast,

While the hail comes hard and fast,

Rattling loud against the glass;

And the snowy sleets, that pass,

Driving up in heaps remain

Close adhering to the pane,

Stop the light, and spread a gloom,

Suiting sleep, around the room :—

Oh, how blest mid these alarms,

I should bask in Fortune's arms,

Who defying every frown,

Hugs me on her downy breast,

Bids my head lie easy down,

And on winter's ruins rest.

So upon the troubled sea,

Emblematic simile,

Birds are known to sit secure,

While the billows roar and rave,

Slumbering in their safety sure,

Rock'd to sleep upon the wave.

So would I still slumber on,

Till hour-telling clocks had gone,

And from the contracted day,

One or more had click'd away.

Then with sitting wearied out,

I for change's sake, no doubt,

Just might wish to leave my seat,

And to exercise my feet,

Make a journey to the door,

Put my nose out, but no more;

There to village taste agree,

Mark how times are like to be,

How the weather's getting on,

Peep in ruts where carts have gone,

Or, by stones, a sturdy stroke,

View the hole the boys have broke:

Then, to pause on ills to come,

Just look upward on the gloom;

See fresh storms approaching fast,

View them busy in the air,

Boiling up the brewing blast;

Still fresh horrors scheming there.

Black and dismal rising high,

From the north they fright the eye

Pregnant with a thousand storms,

Huddled in their icy arms,

Heavy hovering as they come,

Some as mountains seem—and some

Jagg'd as craggy rocks appear,

Dismally advancing near :

Fancy, at the cumbrous sight,

Chills and shudders with affright,

Fearing lest the air, in vain,

Strives her station to maintain,

And wearied, yielding to the skies,

The world beneath in ruin lies.

So may fancy think and feign ;

Fancy oft imagines vain :

Nature's laws by wisdom penn'd,

Mortals cannot comprehend ;

Power almighty Being gave,

Endless Mercy stoops to save ;

Causes, hid from mortals' sight,

Prove " whatever is, is right."

Then to look again below,

Labour's former life I'd view,

Who, still beating through the snow,

Spite of storms their toils pursue,

Forc'd out by sad necessity,

That sad fiend that forces me.

Troubles, then no more my own,

Which I but too long had known,

Might create a care, a pain;

Then I'd seek my joys again:

Pile the fire up, fetch a drink,

Then sit down again and think;

Pause on all my sorrows past,

Think how many a bitter blast,

When it snow'd, and hail'd, and blew,

I have toil'd and batter'd through.

Then to ease reflective pain,

To my sports I'd fall again,

Till the clock had counted ten;

When I'd seek my downy bed,

Easy, happy, and well fed.

D 3

Then might peep the morn in vain,

Through the rimy misted pane;

Then might bawl the restless cock,

And the loud-tongued village clock;

And the flail might lump away,

Waking soon the dreary day:

They should never waken me,

Independent, blest, and free;

Nor, as usual, make me start,

Yawning sigh with heavy heart,

Loth to ope my sleepy eyes,

Weary still, in pain to rise,

With aching bones and heavy head

Worse than when I went to bed.

With nothing then to raise a sigh,

Oh how happy should I lie

Till the clock was eight, or more,

Then proceed as heretofore.

Best of blessings! sweetest charm!

Boon these wishes while they're warm;

My fairy visions ne'er despise;
As reason thinks, thou realize:
Depress'd with want and poverty,
I sink, I fall, denied by thee.

THE FOUNTAIN.

HER dusky mantle Eve had spread;
The west sky glower'd with copper red;
  Sun bid " good night," and slove to bed
'Hind black cloud's mimick'd mountain;
  When weary from my toil I sped,
To seek the purling fountain.

Labour had gi'en it up for good,
Save swains their folds that beetling stood,
  While Echo list'ning in the wood,
Each knock kept 'stinctly counting;
  The Moon just peep'd her horned hood,
Faint glimmering in the fountain.

Ye gently dimpled, curling streams,
Rilling as smooth as summer dreams,
  Ill pair'd to yours life's current seems,
When Hope, rude cataracts mounting,
  Bursts cheated into vain extremes,
Far from the peaceful fountain.

I'd just streak'd down, and with a swish
Whang'd off my hat soak'd like a fish,
  When 'bove what heart could think or wish—
For chance there's no accounting—
  A sweet lass came with wooden dish,
And dipt it in the fountain.

I've often found a rural charm
In pastoral song my heart to warm,
　But, faith, her beauties gave alarm,
'Bove all I'd seen surmounting;
　And when to the spring she stretch'd her arm
My heart chill'd in the fountain.

Simple, witching, artless maid,
So modestly she offer'd aid,
　" And will you please to drink?" she said;
My pulse beat past the counting;
　Oh! Innocence such charms display'd,
I can't forget the fountain.

Ere, lonely, home she 'gan proceed,
I said—what's secrecy indeed,
　And offer'd company as need,
The moon was highly mounting;
　And still her charms—I'd scorn the deed—
Were pure as was the fountain.

Ye leaning palms, that seem to look

Pleas'd o'er your image in the brook;

  Ye ashes, harbouring pye and rook,

Your shady boughs be mounting;

  Ye Muses, leave Castalia's nook

And sacred make the fountain.

TO AN INSIGNIFICANT FLOWER,

OBSCURELY BLOOMING IN A LONELY WILD.

AND though thou seem'st a weedling wild,

  Wild and neglected like to me;

Thou still art dear to nature's child,

  And I will stoop to notice thee.

For oft, like thee, in wild retreat,
  Array'd in humble garb like thee,
There's many a seeming weed proves sweet,
  As sweet as garden-flowers can be.

And, like to thee, each seeming weed
  Flowers unregarded, like to thee
Without improvement runs to seed,
  Wild and neglected like to me.

And, like to thee, when beauty's cloth'd
  In lowly raiment, like to thee;
Disdainful pride, by beauty loath'd,
  No beauties there can ever see.

For, like to thee, my Emma blows,
  A flower like thee I dearly prize;
And, like to thee, her humble clothes
  Hide every charm from prouder eyes.

But though, like thee, a lowly flower,
   If fancied by a polish'd eye,
She soon would bloom beyond my power,
   The finest flower beneath the sky.

And, like to thee, lives many a swain
   With genius blest; but, like to thee,
So humble, lowly, mean, and plain,
   No one will notice them, or me.

So, like to thee, they live unknown,
   Wild weeds obscure; and, like to thee,
Their sweets are sweet to them alone:
   The only pleasure known to me.

Yet when I'm dead, let's hope I have
   Some friend in store, as I'm to thee,
That will find out my lowly grave,
   And heave a sigh to notice me.

ELEGY ON THE RUINS OF PICKWORTH,

RUTLANDSHIRE.

HASTILY COMPOSED, AND WRITTEN WITH A PENCIL ON THE SPOT.

THESE buried ruins, now in dust forgot,
  These heaps of stone the only remnants seen,—
" The Old Foundations" still they call the spot,
  Which plainly tells inquiry what has been—

A time was once, though now the nettle grows
  In triumph o'er each heap that swells the ground,
When they, in buildings pil'd, a village rose,
  With here a cot, and there a garden crown'd.

And here while grandeur, with unequal share,
  Perhaps maintain'd its idleness and pride,
Industry's cottage rose contented there,
  With scarce so much as wants of life supplied.

Mysterious cause! still more mysterious plann'd,
  (Although undoubtedly the will of Heaven:)
To think what careless and unequal hand
  Metes out each portion that to man is given.

While vain extravagance, for one alone,
  Claims half the land his grandeur to maintain;
What thousands, not a rood to call their own,
  Like me but labour for support in vain?

Here we see Luxury surfeit with excess;
  There Want, bewailing, beg from door to door;
Still meeting sorrow where he meets success,
  By lengthening life that liv'd in vain before.

Ye scenes of desolation spread around,
  Prosperity to you did once belong;
And, doubtless, where these brambles claim the
     ground,
The glass once flow'd to hail the ranting song.

The ale-house here might stand, each hamlet's boast;

　　And here, where alder rich from ruin grows,

The tempting sign—but what was once is lost:

　　Who would be proud of what this world bestows?

How Contemplation mourns their lost decay,

　　To view their pride laid level with the ground;

To see, where labour clears the soil away,

　　What fragments of mortality abound.

There's not a rood of land demands our toil,

　　There's not a foot of ground we daily tread,

But gains increase from time's devouring spoil,

　　But holds some fragment of the human dead.

The very food, which for support we have,

　　Claims for its share an equal portion too;

The dust of many a long-forgotten grave

　　Serves to manure the soil from whence it grew.

Since first these ruins fell, how chang'd the scene!

What busy, bustling mortals now unknown,

Have come and gone, as though there nought had

been,

Since first Oblivion call'd the spot her own.

Ye busy, bustling mortals, known before,

Of what you've done, where went, or what you see,

Of what your hopes attain'd to, (now no more,)

For everlasting lies a mystery.

Like yours, awaits for me that common lot;

'Tis mine to be of every hope bereft:

A few more years and I shall be forgot,

And not a vestige of my memory left.

NOON.

ALL how silent and how still,

Nothing heard but yonder mill;

While the dazzled eye surveys

All around a liquid blaze;

And amid the scorching gleams,

If we earnest look, it seems

As if crooked bits of glass

Seem'd repeatedly to pass.

Oh, for a puffing breeze to blow;

But breezes are all strangers now ·

Not a twig is seen to shake,

Nor the smallest bent to quake;

From the river's muddy side,

Not a curve is seen to glide;

And no longer on the stream,

Watching lies the silver bream,

Forcing, from repeated springs,

" Verges in successive rings."

Bees are faint, and cease to hum,

Birds are overpower'd and dumb.

Rural voices all are mute,

Tuneless lie the pipe and flute :

Shepherds with their panting sheep,

In the swaliest corner creep,

And from the tormenting heat

All are wishing to retreat.

Huddled up in grass and flowers,

Mowers wait for cooler hours ;

And the cow-boy seeks the sedge,

Ramping in the woodland hedge,

While his cattle o'er the vales

Scamper with uplifted tails ;

Others not so wild and mad,

That can better bear the gad,

Underneath the hedge-row lunge,

Or, if nigh, in waters plunge.

Oh! to see how flowers are took,

How it grieves me when I look:

Ragged-robins, once so pink,

Now are turn'd as black as ink,

And the leaves being scorch'd so much,

Even crumble at the touch;

Drowking lies the meadow-sweet,

Flopping down beneath one's feet:

While to all the flowers that blow,

If in open air they grow,

Th' injurious deed alike is done

By the hot relentless sun.

E'en the dew is parched up

From the teazle's jointed cup:

O poor birds! where must ye fly,

Now your water-pots are dry?

If ye stay upon the heath,

Ye'll be choak'd and clamm'd to death:

Therefore leave the shadeless goss,

Seek the spring-head lin'd with moss;

There your little feet may stand,

Safely printing on the sand ;

While, in full possession, where

Purling eddies ripple clear,

You with ease and plenty blest,

Sip the coolest and the best.

Then away! and wet your throats ;

Cheer me with your warbling notes ;

'Twill hot noon the more revive ;

While I wander to contrive

For myself a place as good,

In the middle of a wood :

There aside some mossy bank,

Where the grass in bunches rank

Lifts its down on spindles high,

Shall be where I'll choose to lie ;

Fearless of the things that creep,

There I'll think, and there I'll sleep ;

Caring not to stir at all,

Till the dew begins to fall,

THE VILLAGE FUNERAL.

To yon low church, with solemn sounding knell,
    Which t'other day, as rigid fate decreed,
Mournfully knoll'd a widow's passing bell,
    The village funeral's warned to proceed.

Mournful indeed! the orphans' friends are fled:
    Their father's tender care has long been past;
The widow's toil was all their hope of bread,
    And now the grave awaits to seize the last.

But that providing Power, for ever nigh,
    The universal friend of all distress,
Is sure to hear their supplicating cry,
    And prove a father to the fatherless.

E

Now from the low, mud cottage on the moor,
  By two and two sad bend the weeping train;
The coffin, ready near the propt-up door,
  Now slow proceeds along the wayward lane.

While, as they nearer draw in solemn state,
  The village neighbours are assembled round;
And seem with fond anxiety to wait
  The sad procession in the burial ground.

Yet every face the face of sorrow wears;
  And now the solemn scene approaches nigh,
Each to make way for the slow march prepares,
  And on the coffin casts a serious eye.

Now walks the curate through the silent crowd,
  In snowy surplice loosely banded round;
Now meets the corse, and now he reads aloud
  In mournful tone along the burial ground.

The church they enter, and adown the aisle,
  Which more than usual wears a solemn hue,
They rest the coffin on set forms awhile,
  Till the good priest performs the office due.

And though by duty aw'd to silence here,
  The orphans' griefs so piercing force a way;
And, oh! so moving do their griefs appear,
  The worthy pastor kneels, in tears, to pray.

The funeral rites perform'd, by custom thought
  A tribute sacred and essential here,
Now to the last, last place the body's brought,
  Whence all, dread fate! are summon'd to appear.

The church-yard round a mournful view displays,
  Views where mortality is plainly penn'd;
Drear seem the objects which the eye surveys,
  As objects pointing to our latter end.

There the lank nettles sicken ere they seed,
   Where from old trees eve's cordial vainly falls
To raise or comfort each dejected weed,
   While pattering drops decay the crumbling walls.

Here stand, far distant from the pomp of pride,
   Mean little stones, thin scatter'd here and there;
By the scant means of Poverty applied,
   The fond memorial of her friends to bear.

O Memory! thou sweet, enliv'ning power,
   Thou shadow of that fame all hope to find;
The meanest soul exerts her utmost power,
   To leave some fragment of a name behind.

Now crowd the sad spectators round to see
   The deep sunk grave, whose heap of swelling mold,
Full of the fragments of mortality,
   Makes the heart shudder while the eyes behold.

Aw'd is the mind, by dreaded truths imprest,

    To think that dust, which they before them see,

Once liv'd like them : chill Conscience tells the rest,—

    That, like that dust, themselves must shortly be.

The gaping grave now claims its destin'd prey,

    " Ashes to ashes—dust to dust," is given ;

The parent earth receives her kindred clay,

    And the soul starts to meet its home in heaven.

Ah, helpless babes ! now grief in horror shrieks,

    Now sorrow pauses dumb : each looker-on

Knows not the urging language which it speaks,—

    A friend—provider—this world's all—is gone !

Envy and malice now have lost their aim,

    Slander's reproachful tongue can rail no more ;

Her foes now pity where they us'd to blame ;

    The faults and foibles of this life are o'er.

The orphans' grief and sorrow, so severe,
   To every heart in pity's language speak;
E'en the rough sexton can't withhold the tear,
   That steals unnótic'd down his furrow'd cheek.

Who but is griev'd to see the fatherless
   Stroll with their rags unnotic'd through the street?
What eye but moistens at their sad distress,
   And sheds compassion's tear whene'er they meet?

Yon workhouse stands as their asylum now,
   The place where poverty demands to live;
Where parish bounty scowls his scornful brow,
   And grudges the scant fare he's forc'd to give.

Oh, may I die before I'm doom'd to seek
   That last resource of hope, but ill supplied;
To claim the humble pittance once a week,
   Which justice forces from disdainful pride!—

Where the lost orphan, lowly bending, weeps,

    Unnotic'd by the heedless as they pass,

There the grave closes where a mother sleeps,

    With brambles platted on the tufted grass.

EARLY RISING.

JUST at the early peep of dawn,

While brushing through the dewy lawn,

And viewing all the sweets of morn

           That shine at early rising;

Ere the ploughman yok'd his team,

Or sun had power to gild the stream,

Or woodlarks 'gan their morning hymn

           To hail its early rising;

With modest look and bashful eye,

Artless, innocent, and shy,

A lovely maiden pass'd me by,

   And charm'd my early rising.

Her looks had every power to wound,

Her voice had music in the sound,

When modestly she turn'd around

   To greet my early rising.

Good nature forc'd the maid to speak;

And good behaviour, not to seek,

Gave sweetness to her rosy cheek,

   Improv'd by early rising.

While brambles caught her passing by,

And her fine leg engag'd my eye,

Oh, who could paint confusion's dye,

   The blush of early rising!

While offering help to climb the stile,
A modest look and winning smile
(Love beaming in her eyes the while)
   Repaid my early rising.

Aside the green hill's steepy brow,
Where shades the oak its darksome bough,
The maiden sat to milk her cow,
   The cause of early rising.

The wild rose mingling with the shade,
Stung with envy, clos'd to fade,
To see the rose her cheeks display'd,
   The fruits of early rising.

The kiss desir'd—against her will,
To take the milk-pail up the hill,—
Seem'd from resistance sweeter still :
   Thrice happy early rising !

3 E

And often since, aside the grove,

I've hied to meet the girl I love;

Repeating truths that time shall prove,

          Which past at early rising.

May it be mine to spend my days

With her, whose beauty claims my praise;

Then joy shall crown my rural lays,

          And bless my early rising.

MY MARY.

WHO lives where beggars rarely speed,

And leads a hum-drum life indeed,

As none beside herself would lead?

          My Mary.

Who lives where noises never cease,

And what wi' hogs, and ducks, and geese,

Can never have a minute's peace?

My Mary.

Who, nearly battled to her chin,

Bangs down the yard through thick and thin,

Nor picks her road, nor cares a pin?

My Mary.

Who, save in Sunday's bib and tuck,

Goes daily waddling like a duck,

O'er head and ears in grease and muck?

My Mary.

Unus'd to pattens or to clogs,

Who takes the swill to serve the hogs,

And steals the milk for cats and dogs?

My Mary.

Who, frost and snow, as hard as nails,

Stands out o' doors, and never fails

To wash up things and scour the pails?

> My Mary.

Who bustles night and day, in short,

At all catch jobs of every sort,

And gains her mistress' favour for't?

> My Mary.

And who is oft repaid with praise,

In doing what her mistress says,

And yielding to her whimmy ways?

> My Mary.

For there's none apter, I believe,

At " creeping up a mistress' sleeve,"

Than this low kindred stump of Eve,

> My Mary.

Who when the baby's all ——,

To please its mamma kisses it,

And vows no rose on earth's so sweet ?

                        My Mary.

But when her mistress is not nigh,

Who swears, and wishes it would die,

And pinches it and makes it cry ?

                        My Mary.

Oh, rank deceit ! what soul could think—

But gently there, revealing ink :

At faults of thine thy friend must wink,

                        My Mary.

Who, not without a " spark o' pride,"

Though strong as grunter's bristly hide,

Doth keep her hair in papers tied ?

                        My Mary.

And, mimicking the gentry's way,

Who strives to speak as fine as they,

And minds but every word they say?

                My Mary.

And who, though's well bid blind to see,

As her to tell ye A from **B**,

Thinks herself none o' low degree?

                My Mary.

Who prates and runs o'er silly stuff,

And 'mong the boys makes sport enough,

So ugly, silly, droll and rough?

                My Mary.

Ugly! Muse, for shame of thee,

What faults art thou a going to see

In one, that's 'lotted out to be

                My Mary?

Who low in stature, thick and fat,

Turns brown from going without a hat,

Though not a pin the worse for that?

> My Mary.

Who's laugh'd at too by every whelp,

For failings which she cannot help?

But silly fools will laugh and chelp,

> My Mary.

For though in stature mighty small,

And near as thick as thou art tall,

The hand made thee, that made us all,

> My Mary.

And though thy nose hooks down too much,

And prophesies thy chin to touch;

I'm not so nice to look at such,

> My Mary.

No, no; about thy nose and chin,

Its hooking out, or bending in,

I never heed or care a pin,

>   My Mary.

And though thy skin is brown and rough,

And form'd by nature hard and tough,

All suiteth me! so that's enough,

>   My Mary.

—◆—

TO A ROSE-BUD IN HUMBLE LIFE.

SWEET, uncultivated blossom,

>   Rear'd in spring's refreshing dews,

Dear to every gazer's bosom,

>   Fair to every eye that views;

Opening bud, whose youth can charm us,

  Thine be many a happy hour;

Spreading rose, whose beauty warms us,

  Flourish long, my lovely flower!

Though pride looks disdainful on thee,

  Scorning scenes so mean as thine,

Although fortune frowns upon thee,

  Lovely blossom, ne'er repine;

Health unbought is ever wi' thee,

  What their wealth can never gain;

Innocence doth garments gi'e thee,

  Such as fashion apes in vain.

When fit time and reason grant thee

  Leave to quit thy parent tree,

May some happy hand transplant thee

  To a station suiting thee:

On some lover's worthy bosom,

    May'st thou then thy sweets resign;

And may each unfolding blossom

    Open charms as sweet as thine.

Till that time, may joys unceasing

    Thy bard's every wish fulfil;

When that's come, may joys increasing

    Make thee blest and happier still:

Flourish fair, thou flower of Jessys;

    Pride of each admiring swain;

Envy of despairing lasses;

    Queen of Walkherd's lonely plain.

THE UNIVERSAL EPITAPH.

No flattering praises daub my stone,
   My frailties and my faults to hide;
My faults and failings all are known—
   I liv'd in sin—in sin I died.
And oh! condemn me not, I pray,
   You who my sad confession view;
But ask your soul, if it can say,
   That I'm a viler man than you.

FAMILIAR EPISTLE,

TO A FRIEND.

" Friendship, peculiar boon of heav'n,
The noblest mind's delight and pride;
To men and angels only giv'n,
To all the lower world denied :
Thy gentle flows of guiltless joys
On fools and villains ne'er descend,
In vain for thee the tyrant sighs,
And hugs a flatterer for a friend."

JOHNSON.

THIS morning, just as I awoken,

A black cloud hung the south unbroken;

Thinks I, just now we'll have it soakin' ·

  I rightly guess'd.

'Faith! glad were I to see the token,

  I wanted rest.

And, 'fex! a pepp'ring day there's been on't;
But caution'd right with what I'd seen on't,
Keeping at home has kept me clean on't;
        Ye know my creed:
Fool-hardy work, I ne'er was keen on't—
        But let's proceed.

I write to keep from mischief merely,
Fire-side comforts 'joying cheerly;
And, brother chip, I love ye dearly,
        Poor as ye be!
With honest heart and soul, sincerely,
        They're all to me.

This scrawl, mark thou the application,
Though hardly worth thy observation,
Meaneth an humble invitation
        On some day's end:
Of all ragg'd-muffins in the nation,
        Thou art the friend.

I've long been aggravated shocking,
To see our gentry folks so cocking :
But sorrow's often catch'd by mocking,
          The truth I've seen ;
Their pride may want a shoe or stocking,
          For like has been.

Pride's power's not worth a roasted onion
I'd's lief be prison mouse wi' Bunyan,
As I'd be king of our dominion,
          Or any other,
When shuffled through ; it's my opinion,
          One's good as t'other.

Nor would I gie from off my cuff,
A single pin for all such stuff :
Riches ! rubbish ! a pinch of snuff
          Would dearly buy ye;
Who's got ye, keeps ye, that's enough :
          I don't envy ye.

If fate's so kind to let's be doing,

That's—just keep cart on wheels a going;

O'er my half-pint I can be crowing,

      As well's another:

But when there's this and that stands owing,

      O curse the bother!

For had I money, like a many,

I'd balance, even to a penny.

Want! thy confinement makes me scranny ·

      That spirit's mine,

I'd sooner gi'e than take from any;

      But worth can't shine.

O Independence! oft I bait ye;

How blest I'd be to call ye matey!

Ye fawning, flattering slaves I hate ye:

      · Mad, harum-scarum !

If rags and tatters under-rate me,

      Free still I'll wear 'em.

But hang all sorrows, now I'll bilk 'em;
What's past shall go so: time that shall come,
Or bad, or worse, or how it will come,
        I'll ne'er despair;
Poor as I am, friends shall be welcome
        As rich men's are.

So from my heart, old friend, I'll greet ye:
No outside brags shall ever cheat ye;
Wi' what I have, wi' such I'll treat ye,
        Ye may believe me;
I'll shake your rags whene'er I meet ye,
        If ye deceive me.

So mind ye, friend, what's what, I send it:
My letter's plain, and plain I'll end it:
Bad's bad enough, but worse won't mend it;
        So I'll be happy,
And while I've sixpence left I'll spend it
        In cheering nappy.

A hearty health shall crown my story :—
Dear, native England! I adore ye;
Britons, may ye with friends before ye
     Ne'er want a quart,
To drink your king and country's glory
     Wi' upright heart!

POSTSCRIPT.

I've oft meant tramping o'er to see ye;
But, d—d old Fortune, (God forgi'e me!)
She's so cross-grain'd and forked wi' me,
     Be e'er so willing,
With all my jingling powers 'tint i' me
     To scheme a shilling.

And Poverty, with cursed rigour,
Spite of industry's utmost vigour,
Dizens me out in such a figure
     I'm sham'd being seen;
'Sides my old shoon, (poor Muse, ye twig her,)
     Wait roads being clean.

F

Then here wind-bound till Fate's conferr'd on't,

I wait ye, friend; and take my word on't,

I'll, spite of fate, scheme such a hoard on't,

   As we won't lack:

So no excuses shall be heard on't.

   Yours, random Jack.

THE HARVEST MORNING.

Cocks wake the early morn with many a crow;

Loud striking village clock has counted four;

The labouring rustic hears his restless foe,

And weary, of his pains complaining sore,

Hobbles to fetch his horses from the moor:

Some busy 'gin to team the loaded corn

Which night throng'd round the barn's becrowded

  door.

Such plenteous scenes the farmer's yard adorn,

Such noisy, busy toils now mark the harvest morn.

The bird-boy's pealing horn is loudly blow'd;

The waggons jostle on with rattling sound;

And hogs and geese now throng the dusty road,

Grunting and gabbling, in contention, round

The barley ears that litter on the ground.

What printing traces mark the waggon's way;

What dusty bustling wakens echo round;

How drive the sun's warm beams the mist away;

How labour sweats and toils, and dreads the sultry
     day!

His scythe the mower o'er his shoulder leans,

And whetting, jars with sharp and tinkling sound,

Then sweeps again 'mong corn and crackling beans,

And swath by swath flops lengthening o'er the
     ground;

While 'neath some friendly heap, snug shelter'd
     round

From spoiling sun, lies hid the heart's delight;

And hearty soaks oft hand the bottle round,

Their toils pursuing with redoubled might
Great praise to him be due that brought its birth to
    light.

Upon the waggon now, with eager bound,
The lusty picker whirls the rustling sheaves;
Or, resting ponderous creaking fork aground,
Boastful at once whole shocks of barley heaves:
The loading boy revengeful inly grieves
To find his unmatch'd strength and power decay;
The barley horn his garments interweaves;
Smarting and sweating 'neath the sultry day,
With muttering curses stung, he mauls the heaps
    away.

A motley group the clearing field surrounds:
Sons of humanity, oh ne'er deny
The humble gleaner entrance in your grounds;
Winter's sad cold, and Poverty are nigh.
Grudge not from Providence the scant supply:

You'll never miss it from your ample store.

Who gives denial,—harden'd, hungry hound,—

May never blessings crowd his hated door!

But he shall never lack, that giveth to the poor.

Ah, lovely Emma! mingling with the rest,

Thy beauties blooming in low life unseen,

Thy rosy cheeks, thy sweetly swelling breast;

But ill it suits thee in the stubs to glean.

O Poverty! how basely you demean

The imprison'd worth your rigid fates confine;

Not fancied charms of an Arcadian queen,

So sweet as Emma's real beauties shine:

Had Fortune blest, sweet girl, this lot had ne'er

been thine.

The sun's increasing heat now mounted high,

Refreshment must recruit exhausted power;

The waggon stops, the busy tool's thrown by,

And 'neath a shock's enjoy'd the bevering hour.

The bashful maid, sweet health's engaging flower,

Lingering behind, o'er rake still blushing bends;

And when to take the horn fond swains implore,

With feign'd excuses its dislike pretends.

So pass the bevering hours, so harvest morning ends.

O rural life! what charms thy meanness hide;

What sweet descriptions bards disdain to sing;

What loves, what graces on thy plains abide:

Oh, could I soar me on the Muse's wing,

What rifled charms should my researches bring!

Pleas'd would I wander where these charms
        reside;

Of rural sports and beauties would I sing;

Those beauties, Wealth, which you in vain deride,

Beauties of richest bloom, superior to your pride.

ON BEAUTY.

———

BEAUTY, how changing and how frail!
　　As skies in April showers,
Or as the summer's minute-gales,
　　Or as the morning flowers.

As April skies, so beauty shades;
　　As summer gales, so beauty flies;
As morning flower at evening fades,
　　So beauty's tender blossom dies.

ON AN INFANT'S GRAVE.

BENEATH the sod where smiling creep
   The daisies into view,
The ashes of an infant sleep,
   Whose soul's as smiling too;
Ah! doubly happy, doubly blest,
   (Had I so happy been!)
Recall'd to heaven's eternal rest,
   Ere it knew how to sin.

Thrice happy infant! great the bliss
   Alone reserv'd for thee;
Such joy 'twas my sad fate to miss,
   And thy good luck to see;

For oh ! when all must rise again,
    And sentence then shall have,
What crowds will wish with me, in vain,
    They'd fill'd an infant's grave.

DOLLY'S MISTAKE;

OR, THE WAYS OF THE WAKE.

ERE the sun o'er the lulls, round and red, 'gan a
    peeping,
    To beckon the chaps to their ploughs,
Too thinking and restless all night to be sleeping,
    I brush'd off to milking my cows ;
To get my jobs forward, and eager preparing
    To be off in time to the wake,
Where yielding so freely a kiss for a fairing,
    I made a most shocking mistake.

Young Ralph met me early, and off we were steering,
  I cuddled me close to his side;
The neighbours, while passing, my fondness kept
      jeering,
  " Young Ralph's timely suited !" they cried.
But he bid me mind not their evil pretensions,
  " Fools mun," says he, " talk for talk's sake;"
And, kissing me, " Doll, if you've any 'prehensions,
  " Let me tell you, my wench, you mistake."

My cows when we pass'd them kept booing and
      mooing,
  In truth, but they made me to stare;
As much as to say, " Well, now, Dolly, you're going,
  Mind how you get on at the fair."
While bidden " good speed" from each gazing be-
      holder,
  " Good journey away to the wake,"
The mowers stopp'd whetting, to look o'er their
      shoulder,
  Saying, " Dolly, don't make a mistake."

I couldn't but mind the fine morning so charming,

 The dew-drops they glitter'd like glass;

And all o'er the meads were the buttercups swarm-

  ing,

 Like so many suns in the grass:

I thought as we pass'd them, if such a thing could

  be,

 What a fine string of beads they would make;

But when I could think of such nonsense, it would be

 Because I had made no mistake.

So on his arm hanging, with stories beguiling,

 Of what he would buy me when there,

The road cutting short with his kissing and smiling,

 He 'veigl'd me off to the fair:

Such presents he proffer'd before I could claim 'em,

 To keep while I liv'd for his sake,

And what I lik'd best, o'er and o'er begg'd me name

  'em,

 That he mightn't go make a mistake.

And, lud, what a crushing and crowding were wi'
    'em,
  What noises are heard at a fair;
Here some sell so cheap, as they'd even go gi' 'em,
  If conscience would take, they declare :
Some so good, 'tis e'en worth more than money to
    buy 'em,
  Fine gingerbread nuts and plum-cake ;
For truth they bid Ralph, ere he treated me, try 'em,
  And then there could be no mistake.

A sly Merry Andrew was making his speeches,
  With chaps and girls round him a swarm,
And, " Mind," said he, fleering, " ye chubby-fac'd
    witches,
  Your fairings don't do you some harm."
The hay-cocks he nam'd, in the meads passing by 'em,
  When weary we came from the wake,
So soft, so inviting, for rest we mun try 'em ;
  What a fool should I be to mistake.

But promis'd so faithful, behaviour so clever,
 Such gifts as Ralph cramm'd in my hand,
How could I distrust of his goodness? O never!
 And who could his goodness withstand?
His ribbons, his fairings, past counting, or nearly,
 Some return when he press'd me to make,
Good manners mun give, while he lov'd me so
  dearly ·
 Ah! where could I see the mistake?

'Till dark night he kept me, with fussing and lying,
 How he'd see me safe home to my cot;
Poor maiden, so easy, so free in complying,
 I the showman's good caution forgot:
All bye-ways he led me, 'twas vain to dispute it,
 The moon blush'd for shame, naughty rake!
Behind a cloud sneaking—but darkness well
  suited
 His baseness, who caus'd the mistake.

In vain do I beg him to wed and have done wi't,
    So fair as he promis'd we should;
We cou'dn't do worse than as how we've begun wi't,
    Let matters turn out as they would:
But he's always a talking 'bout wedding expenses,
    And the wages he's gotten to take;
Too plain can I see through his evil pretences,
    Too late I find out the mistake.

Oh, what mun I do with my mother reprovin',
    Since she will do nothing but chide?
For when old transgressors have been in the oven,
    They know where the young ones may hide.
In vain I seek pity with plaints and despairings,
    Always ding'd on the nose with the wake:
Young maidens! be cautious who give you your
        fairings;
    Ye see what attends a mistake.

ON CRUELTY

COMPASSION sighs, and feels, and weeps,
    Retracing every pain
Inhuman man, in vengeance, heaps
    On all the lower train.

Ah, Pity! oft thy heart has bled,
    As galling now it bleeds;
And tender tears thy eyes have shed
    To witness cruel deeds.

The lash that weal'd poor Dobbin's hide,
    The strokes that cracking fall
On dogs, dumb cringing by thy side—
    Ah! thou hast felt them all.

The burthen'd asses, 'mid the laugh
   To see them whipp'd, would move
Thy soul to breathe in their behalf
   Humanity and love.

E'en 'plaining flies to thee have spoke,
   Poor trifles as they be;
And oft the spider's web thou'st broke,
   To set the captive free.

The pilfering mouse, entrapp'd and cag'd
   Within the wiry grate,
Thy pleading powers has oft engag'd
   To mourn its rigid fate.

How beat thy breast with conscious woes,
   To see the sparrows die:
Poor little thieves of many foes,
   Their food they dearly buy.

Where nature groans, where nature cries
  Beneath the butcher's knife,
How vain, how many were thy sighs,
  To save such guiltless life.

And ah! that most inhuman plan,
  Where reason's name's ador'd,
Unfriendly treatment—man to man—
  Thy tears have oft deplor'd.

Nor wise, nor good shall e'er deride
  The tear in Pity's eye;
Though laugh'd to scorn by senseless pride,
  From them it meets a sigh.

ON THE DEATH OF A BEAUTIFUL YOUNG LADY.

YE meaner beauties cease your pride,
  Where borrow'd charms adorn;
Here nature aid of art defied,
  And blossom'd all its own.

The rose your paint but idly feigns,
  Bloom'd nature's brightest dyes;
The gems your wealthy pride sustains,
  Were natives of her eyes.

But what avails superior charms
  To boast of when in power,
Since, subject to a thousand harms,
  They perish like a flower.

Alas! we've nought to boast of here,
 And less to make us proud;
The brightest sun but rises clear
 To set behind a cloud.

Those charms which every heart subdue,
 Must all their powers resign;
Those eyes, like suns, too bright to view,
 Have now forgot to shine.

Her beauties so untimely fell,
 What mortal would be proud?
The day return'd, and found her well,
 But left her in her shroud.

To day the blossom buds and blooms,
 But who a day can trust?
Since the to-morrow, when it comes,
 Condemns it to the dust.

FALLING LEAVES.

HAIL, falling leaves! that patter round,
  Admonishers and friends;
Reflection wakens at the sound—
  So, Life, thy pleasure ends.

How frail the bloom, how short the stay,
  That terminates us all !
To day we flourish green and gay,
  Like leaves to-morrow fall.

Alas! how short is fourscore years,
  Life's utmost stretch,—a span;
And shorter still, when past, appears
  The vain, vain life of man.

These falling leaves once flaunted high,
  O pride! how vain to trust:
Now wither'd on the ground they lie,
  And mingled with the dust.

So death serves all—and wealth and pride
  Must all their pomp resign ;
E'en kings shall lay their crowns aside,
  To mix their dust with mine.

The leaves, how once they cloth'd the trees,
  None's left behind to tell;
The branch is naked to the breeze ;
  We know not whence they fell.

A few more years, and I the same
  As they are now, shall be,
With nothing left to tell my name
  Or answer, " Who was he?"

Green turf's allow'd forgotten heap
  Is all that I shall have,
Save that the little daisies creep
  To deck my humble grave.

THE CONTRAST OF BEAUTY AND VIRTUE.

" Beauty's a transitory joy,
" But Virtue's sweets shall never cloy."

As o'er the gay pasture went rocking a clown,
A gay, gaudy butter-cup's gold-fringed gown
  Engag'd his attention, as passing her by;
And rudely to gain her he stooped adown,
  Its beauty so dazzled his eye.

By outside appearance the senseless are caught,
But Beauty's gay triumph is foolish and short ;
  With nothing to gain the attention beside,
Possession soon sickens—and fleet as a thought,
  Beauty slips us forgotten aside.

As snifting and snufting the clodhopper goes,
And finding no sweetness for charming his nose,
  Frail Beauty's delusion soon wearied his eye;
And away the gay flowret he heedlessly throws,
  To wither unnotic'd, and die.

Ye young, giddy wenches ! gay butter-cups ! mind,
So tempting your dresses, your nature so kind,
  Virgin beauty once tasted, no longer endures ;
The charm that should please us, fair Virtue, re-
    sign'd,
  A butter-cup's fortune is yours.

Let modesty's sweetness your blossoms adorn,

Be Virtue your guard, as the rose has her thorn;

   Then as chemists the sweets of the roses secure,—

When Beauty's no more, still to please is your own,

   For Virtue's charms ever endure.

TO AN APRIL DAISY.

WELCOME, old comrade! peeping once again;

   Our meeting 'minds me of a pleasant hour

Spring's pencil pinks thee in that blushy stain,

   And Summer glistens in thy tinty flower.

Hail, beauty's gem! disdaining time nor place;

   Carelessly creeping on the dunghill's side;

Demeanour's softness in thy crimpled face

   Decks thee in beauties unattain'd by pride.

Hail, 'venturer! once again that fearless here
　　Encampeth on the hoar hill's sunny side;
Spring's early messenger! thou'rt doubly dear;
　　And winter's frost by thee is well supplied.

Now winter's frowns shall cease their pelting rage,
　　But winter's woes I need not tell to thee;
Far better luck thy visits well presage,
　　And be it thine and mine that luck to see.

Ah, may thy smiles confirm the hopes they tell;
　　To see thee frost-bit I'd be griev'd at heart;
I meet thee happy, and I wish thee well,
　　Till ripening summer summons us to part.

Then like old mates, or two who've neighbours been,
　　We'll part, in hopes to meet 'nother year;
And o'er thy exit from this changing scene,
　　We'll mix our wishes in a tokening tear.

TO HOPE.

COME, flattering Hope! now woes distress me,
 Thy flattery I desire again;
Again rely on thee to bless me,
 To find thy vainness doubly vain.

Though disappointments vex and fetter,
 And jeering whisper thou art vain;
Still must I rest on thee for better,
 Still hope—and be deceiv'd again.

I can't but listen to thy prattle;
 I still must hug thee to my breast:
Like weaning child that's lost its rattle,
 Without my toy I cannot rest.

AN EFFUSION TO POESY,

ON RECEIVING A DAMP FROM A GENTEEL OPINIONIST IN POETRY, OF SOME SWAY, AS I AM TOLD, IN THE LITERARY WORLD.

———

DESPIS'D, unskill'd, or how I will,

Sweet Poesy! I'll love thee still;

Vain (cheering comfort!) though I be,

I still must love thee, Poesy.

A poor, rude clown, and what of that?

I cannot help the will of fate,

A lowly clown although I be;

Nor can I help it loving thee.

Still must I love thee, sweetest charm!

Still must my soul in raptures warm;

Still must my rudeness pluck the flower,

That's plucked in an evil hour,

While Learning scowls her scornful brow,

And damps my soul—I know not how.

Labour! 'cause thou'rt mean and poor,

Learning spurns thee from her door;

But despise me as she will,

Poesy! I love thee still.

When on pillow'd thorns I weep,

And vainly stretch me down to sleep;

Then, thou charm from heav'n above,

Comfort's cordial dost thou prove:

Then, engaging Poesy!

Then how sweet to talk with thee.

And be despis'd, or how I will,

I cannot help but love thee still.

Endearing charm! vain though I be,

I still must love thee, Poesy.

Still must I! ay, I can't refrain:

Damp'd, despis'd, or scorn'd again,

With vain, unhallowed liberty

Still must I sing thee, Poesy.

And poor, and vain, and press'd beneath

Oppression's scorn although I be,

Still will I bind my simple wreath,

Still will I love thee, Poesy.

THE POET'S WISH.

A WISH will rise in every breast,

For something more than what's possess'd;

Some trifle still, or more or less,

To make complete one's happiness.

And, faith! a wish will oft incline

To harbour in this breast of mine;

And oft old Fortune hears my case,

Told plain as nose upon her face.

But vainly do we beggars plead,

Although not ask'd before we need:

Old Fortune, like sly Farmer Dapple,

Where there's an orchard flings her apple;

But where there's no return to make ye,

She turns her nose up, " Deuce may take ye."

So rich men get their wealth at will,

And beggars—why, they're beggars still.

But 'tis not thoughts of being rich

That make my wishing spirit itch;

'Tis just an independent fate,

Betwixt the little and the great;

No out-o'-the-way nor random wish;

No ladle crav'd for silver dish:

'Tis but a comfortable seat,

While without work both ends would meet.

'Tis just get hand to mouth with ease,

And read, and study as I please:

A little garret, warm and high,

As loves the Muse sublime to fly,

With all my friends encircled round
In golden letters, richly bound;
Dear English poets! luckless fellows,
As born to such, so fate will tell us;
Might I their flow'ry themes peruse,
And be as happy in my Muse,
Like them sublimely high to soar,
Without their fate—so cursed poor!
While one snug room, not over small,
Contain'd my necessary all;
And night and day left me secure
'Mong books, my chiefest furniture;
With littering papers, many a bit
Scrawl'd by the Muse in fancied fit.
And curse upon that routing jade,
My territories to invade,
Who finds me out in evil hour,
To brush, and clean, and scrub, and scour;
And with a dreaded brush or broom
Disturbs my learned lumber-room.

Such busy things I hate to see,

Such troublers ne'er shall trouble me :

Let dust keep gathering on the ground,

And roping cobwebs dangle round ;

Let spiders weave their webs at will ;

Would cash, when wanted, pockets till,

To *pint* it just at my desire,

My drooping Muse with ale inspire,

And fetch at least a roll of bread,

Without a debt to run or dread.

Such comforts, would they were but mine,

To something more I'd ne'er incline ·

But happiest then of happy clowns,

   I'd sing all cares away ;

And pitying monarchs capp'd with crowns,

   I'd see more joys than they.

   Thus wish'd a bard, whom fortune scorns,

To find a rose among the thorns ;

And musing o'er each heavy care,

His pen stuck useless in his hair,

His muse was dampt, nor fir'd his soul,

And still unearn'd his penny roll;

Th' unfinish'd labours of his head

Were listless on the table spread;

When lo! to bid him hope no more,

A rap—an earthquake! jars the door;

His heart drops in his shoes with doubt:

" What fiend has found my lodging out?"

Poor trembling tenants of the quill!—

" Here, sir, I bring my master's bill."—

He heav'd a sigh, and scratch'd his head,

And credit's mouth with promise fed:

Then sat in terror down again,

Invok'd the Muse, and scrigg'd a strain;

A trifling something glad to get,

To earn a dinner, and discharge the debt.

SUMMER EVENING.

The sinking sun is taking leave,
And sweetly gilds the edge of Eve,
While huddling clouds of purple dye
Gloomy hang the western sky.
Crows crowd croaking over head,
Hastening to the woods to bed.
Cooing sits the lonely dove,
Calling home her absent love.
With " Kirchup! kirchup!" 'mong the wheats,
Partridge distant partridge greets;
Beckoning hints to those that roam,
That guide the squander'd covey home.
Swallows check their winding flight,
And twittering on the chimney light.

Round the pond the martins flirt,

Their snowy breasts bedaub'd with dirt,

While the mason, 'neath the slates,

Each mortar-bearing bird awaits ·

By art untaught, each labouring spouse

Curious daubs his hanging house.

Bats flit by in hood and cowl;

Through the barn-hole pops the owl;

From the hedge, in drowsy hum,

Heedless buzzing beetles bum,

Haunting every bushy place,

Flopping in the labourer's face.

Now the snail hath made his ring;

And the moth with snowy wing

Circles round in winding whirls,

Through sweet evening's sprinkled pearls,

On each nodding rush besprent;

Dancing on from bent to bent:

Now to downy grasses clung,

Resting for a while he's hung;

Then, to ferry o'er the stream,

Vanishing as flies a dream;

Playful still his hours to keep,

Till his time has come to sleep;

In tall grass, by fountain head,

Weary then he drops to bed.

From the hay-cock's moisten'd heaps,

Startled frogs take vaunting leaps;

And along the shaven mead,

Jumping travellers, they proceed:

Quick the dewy grass divides,

Moistening sweet their speckled sides;

From the grass or flowret's cup,

Quick the dew-drop bounces up.

Now the blue fog creeps along,

And the bird's forgot his song:

Flowers now sleep within their hoods;

Daisies button into buds;

From soiling dew the butter-cup

Shuts his golden jewels up;

And the rose and woodbine they

Wait again the smiles of day.

'Neath the willow's wavy boughs,

Dolly, singing, milks her cows;

While the brook, as bubbling by,

Joins in murmuring melody.

Dick and Dob, with jostling joll,

Homeward drag the rumbling roll;

Whilom Ralph, for Doll to wait,

Lolls him o'er the pasture gate.

Swains to fold their sheep begin;

Dogs loud barking drive them in.

Hedgers now along the road

Homeward bend beneath their load;

And from the long furrow'd seams,

Ploughmen loose their weary teams ·

Ball, with urging lashes weal'd,

Still so slow to drive a-field,

Eager blundering from the plough,

Wants no whip to drive him now;

At the stable-door he stands,

Looking round for friendly hands

To loose the door its fast'ning pin,

And let him with his corn begin.

Round the yard, a thousand ways,

Beasts in expectation gaze,

Catching at the loads of hay

Passing fodd'rers tug away.

Hogs with grumbling, deaf'ning noise,

Bother round the server boys;

And, far and near, the motley group

Anxious claim their suppering-up.

From the rest, a blest release,

Gabbling home, the quarreling geese

Seek their warm straw-litter'd shed,

And, waddling, prate away to bed.

'Nighted by unseen delay,

Poking hens, that lose their way,

On the hovel's rafters rise,

Slumbering there, the fox's prize.

Now the cat has ta'en her seat,

With her tail curl'd round her feet;

Patiently she sits to watch

Sparrows fighting on the thatch.

Now Doll brings th' expected pails,

And dogs begin to wag their tails;

With strokes and pats they're welcom'd in,

And they with looking wants begin:

Slove in the milk-pail brimming o'er,

She pops their dish behind the door.

Prone to mischief boys are met,

'Neath the eaves the ladder's set,

Sly they climb in softest tread,

To catch the sparrow on his bed;

Massacred, O cruel pride!

Dash'd against the ladder's side.

Curst barbarians! pass me by;

Come not, Turks, my cottage nigh;

Sure my sparrows aie my own,

Let ye then my birds alone.

Come, poor birds! from foes severe

Fearless come, you're welcome here;

My heart yearns at fate like yours,

A sparrow's life's as sweet as ours.

Hardy clowns! grudge not the wheat

Which hunger forces birds to eat:

Your blinded eyes, worst foes to you,

Can't see the good which sparrows do.

Did not poor birds with watching rounds

Pick up the insects from your grounds,

Did they not tend your rising grain,

You then might sow to reap in vain.

Thus Providence, right understood,

Whose end and aim is doing good,

Sends nothing here without its use;

Though ignorance loads it with abuse,

And fools despise the blessing sent,

And mock the Giver's good intent.—

O God, let me what's good pursue,

Let me the same to others do

As I'd have others do to me,
And learn at least humanity.

Dark and darker glooms the sky;
Sleep 'gins close the labourer's eye:
Dobson leaves his greensward seat,
Neighbours where they neighbours meet
Crops to praise, and work in hand,
And battles tell from foreign land.
While his pipe is puffing out,
Sue he's putting to the rout,
Gossiping, who takes delight
To shool her knitting out at night,
And back-bite neighbours 'bout the town—
Who's got new caps, and who a gown,
And many a thing, her evil eye
Can see they don't come honest by.
Chattering at a neighbour's house,
She hears call out her frowning spouse;

Prepar'd to start, she soodles home,

Her knitting twirling o'er her thumb,

As, loth to leave, afraid to stay,

She bawls her story all the way:

The tale so fraught with 'ticing charms,

Her apron folded o'er her arms,

She leaves the unfinished tale, in pain,

To end as evening comes again;

And in the cottage gangs with dread,

To meet old Dobson's timely frown,

Who grumbling sits, prepar'd for bed

While she stands chelping 'bout the town.

The night-wind now, with sooty wings,

In the cotter's chimney sings;

Now, as stretching o'er the bed,

Soft I raise my drowsy head,

Listening to the ushering charms,

That shake the elm tree's mossy arms:

Till sweet slumbers stronger creep,
   Deeper darkness stealing round,
Then, as rock'd, I sink to sleep,
   'Mid the wild wind's lulling sound.

SUMMER MORNING.

THE cocks have now the morn foretold,
   The sun again begins to peep;
The shepherd, whistling to his fold,
   Unpens and frees the captive sheep.

O'er pathless plains, at early hours,
   The sleepy rustic sloomy goes;
The dews, brush'd off from grass and flowers,
   Bemoistening sop his harden'd shoes;

For every leaf that forms a shade,
    And every flowret's silken top,
And every shivering bent and blade,
    Stoops, bowing with a diamond drop.

But soon shall fly those pearly drops,
    The red, round sun advances higher;
And stretching o'er the mountain tops,
    Is gilding sweet the village spire.

Again the bustling maiden seeks
    Her cleanly pail, and eager now,
Rivals the morn with rosy cheeks,
    And hastens off to milk her cow;

While echo tells of Colin near,
    Blithe, whistling o'er the misty hills:
The powerful magic fills her ear,
    And through her beating bosom thrills.

'Tis sweet to meet the morning breeze,

   Or list the giggling of the brook;

Or stretch'd beneath the shade of trees

   Peruse and pause on nature's book;

When nature every sweet prepares

   To entertain our wish'd delay,—

The images which morning wears,

   The wakening charms of early day!

Now let me tread the meadow paths,

   While glittering dew the ground illumes,

As, sprinkled o'er the withering swaths,

   Their moisture shrinks in sweet perfumes;

And hear the beetle sound his horn;

   And hear the skylark whistling nigh,

Sprung from his bed of tufted corn,

   A hailing minstrel in the sky.

First sunbeam, calling night away,
   To see how sweet thy summons seems,
Split by the willow's wavy grey,
   And sweetly dancing on the streams :

How fine the spider's web is spun,
   Unnoticed to vulgar eyes;
Its silk thread glittering in the sun,
   Art's bungling vanity defies.

Roaming while the dewy fields
   'Neath their morning burthen lean;
While its crop my searches shields,
   Sweet I scent the blossom'd bean :

Making oft remarking stops;
   Watching tiny, nameless things,
Climb the grass's spiry tops,
   Ere they try their gauzy wings,

So emerging into light,
   From the ignorant and vain,
Fearful Genius takes her flight,
   Skimming o'er the lowly plain.

Now in gay, green, glossy coat,
   On the shivering, benty baulk,
The free grasshopper chirps his note,
   Bounding on from stalk to stalk.

And the bee at early hours
   Sips the tawny bean's perfumes;
While butterflies infest the flowers,
   Just to shew their glossy plumes.

So industry oft seeks the sweet,
   Which weary labour ought to gain;
And oft the bliss the idle meets,
   And heaven bestows the bliss in vain.

Pleas'd, I list the rural themes
    Heartening up the ploughman's toil;
Urging on the jingling teams,
    As they turn the mellow soil.

Industry's care abounds again,
    As now the peace of night is gone;
Many a murmur wakes the plain,
    Many a waggon rumbles on.

The swallow wheels his circling flight,
    And o'er the water's surface skims;
Then on the cottage chimney lights,
    And twittering chants his morning hymns.

Station'd high, a towering height,
    On the sun-gilt weathercock,
Now the jackdaw takes his flight,
    Frighted by the striking clock.

Snug the weary, watching thrush,
 Sits to prune her speckled breast,
Where the woodbine, round the bush
 Weaving, hides her mortar'd nest;

Till the cows, with hungry low,
 Pick the rank grass from her bower;
Startled then—dead leaves below
 Quick receive the pattering shower.

Now the scythe the morn salutes,
 In the meadow tinkling soon;
While on mellow-tootling flutes
 Sweetly breathes the shepherd's tune.

Where the bank the stream o'erlooks,
 And the wreathing worms are found,
Anglers sit to bait their hooks,
 On the hill with wild thyme crown'd.

H

While the treach'rous watching stork

    With the heedless gudgeon flies,

Bobbing sinks the vanish'd cork,

    And the roach becomes a prize.

'Neath the black-thorn's stunted bush,

    Cropp'd by wanton oxen down,

Whistling o'er each culling rush,

    Cow-boys plat a rural crown.

As slow the hazy mists retire,

    Crampt circle's more distinctly seen;

Thin scatter'd huts, and neighbouring spire,

    Drop in to stretch the bounded scene.

Brisk winds the lighten'd branches shake,

    By pattering, plashing drops confess'd;

And, where oaks dripping shade the lake,

    Print crimpling dimples on its breast.

The misted brook, its edges reek ;
   Sultry Noon is drawing on;
The east has lost its ruddy streak,
   And Morning sweets are almost gone.

Now as Morning takes her leave,
   And while swelter'd nature mourns,
Let me, waiting soothing Eve,
   Seek my cot till she returns.

DAWNINGS OF GENIUS.

GENIUS ! a pleasing rapture of the mind,
A kindling warmth to learning unconfin'd,
Glows in each breast, flutters in every vein,
From art's refinement to th' uncultur'd swain.

Hence is that warmth the lowly shepherd proves,

Pacing his native fields and willow groves;

Hence is that joy, when every scene unfolds,

Which taste endears and latest memory holds;

Hence is that sympathy his heart attends,

When bush and tree companions seem and friends;

Hence is that fondness from his soul sincere,

That makes his native place so doubly dear.

In those low paths which Poverty surrounds,

The rough, rude ploughman, off his fallow-grounds,

(That necessary tool of wealth and pride,)

While moil'd and sweating by some pasture's side,

Will often stoop inquisitive to trace

The opening beauties of a daisy's face;

Oft will he witness, with admiring eyes,

The brook's sweet dimples o'er the pebbles rise;

And often, bent as o'er some magic spell,

He'll pause, and pick his shaped stone and shell

Raptures the while his inward powers inflame,

And joys delight him which he cannot name;

Ideas picture pleasing views to mind,

For which his language can no utterance find;

Increasing beauties, fresh'ning on his sight,

Unfold new charms, and witness more delight;

So while the present please, the past decay,

And in each other, losing, melt away.

Thus pausing wild on all he saunters by,

He feels enraptur'd though he knows not why;

And hums and mutters o'er his joys in vain,

And dwells on something which he can't explain.

The bursts of thought with which his soul's perplex'd,

Are bred one moment, and are gone the next;

Yet still the heart will kindling sparks retain,

And thoughts will rise, and Fancy strive again.

So have I mark'd the dying ember's light,

When on the hearth it fainted from my sight,

With glimmering glow oft redden up again,

And sparks crack'd brightening into life, in vain;

Still lingering out its kindling hope to rise,

Till faint, and fainting, the last twinkle dies.

Dim burns the soul, and throbs the fluttering
    heart,
Its painful, pleasing feelings to impart;
Till by successless sallies wearied quite,
The Memory fails, and Fancy takes her flight.
The wick confin'd within its socket dies,
Borne down and smother'd in a thousand sighs.

TO A COLD BEAUTY,

INSENSIBLE OF LOVE.

ELIZA, farewel! ah, most lovely Eliza,
    So much as thy beauties excel;
So much as I love thee, so much as I prize thee,
    Unfeeling Eliza, farewel!
The heart without feeling, the beauty's but small,
    Though tempting it be to the view;
The warmth of a soul crowns the beauty of all,
    Without it thou'rt nothing—adieu!

Thou Image of Beauty, endeavour is vain
  To warm thee to life and to love,
Could I but the skill of the artist attain,
  And steal thee a soul from above;
Though as fair as the statue he finish'd art thou,
  'Twere folly his plan to pursue;
I would give thee feeling, but cannot tell how;
  I would love thee, dear—but, adieu!

To all that life sweetens eternally lost,
  Where love makes a heaven below,
Thy bosom's congealed in apathy's frost,
  As white and as cold as the snow:
Since no spark of soul its dead tenant can warm,
  Thou Icicle hung on Spring's brow,
I'll turn my sighs from thee to mix with the storm;
  The storm's full as tender as thou.

That heart where no feelings or raptures can dwell,

    Be its owner in person most fair,

Were beauty a bargain to buy or to sell,

    I never would purchase it there ·

So cold to the joys that in sympathy burn,

    Joys none but true love ever knew,

How lost should I be could I prove no return:

    I wish to be happy—adieu!

PATTY.

Ye swampy falls of pasture ground,

    And rushy spreading greens;

Ye rising swells in brambles bound,

    And freedom's wilder'd scenes ·

I've trod ye oft, and love ye dear,

    And kind was fate to let me;

On you I found my all, for here

    'Twas first my Patty met me.

Flow on, thou gently plashing stream,
   O'er weed-beds wild and rank;
Delighted I've enjoy'd my dream
   Upon thy mossy bank:
Bemoistening many a weedy stem,
   I've watch'd thee wind so clearly;
And on thy bank I found the gem
   That makes me love thee dearly.

Thou wilderness, so rudely gay;
   Oft as I seek thy plain,
Oft as I wend my steps away,
   And meet my joys again,
And brush the weaving branches by
   Of briars and thorns so matty;
So oft reflection warms a sigh,—
   Here first I met my Patty.

ON YOUTH.

Ah, youth's sweet joys! why are ye gone astray?
  Fain would I follow could I find a plan:
To my great loss are ye exchang'd away,
  For that sad sorrow-ripening name—a man.
Far distant joys! the prospect gives me pain:
  Ah, happiness! and hast thou no return?
No kind concern to call thee back again,
  And bid this aching bosom cease to mourn?
The daisies' hopes have met another Spring,
  Poor standard tenants on a stormy plain;
The lark confirms it on his russet wing;
  And why alone am I denied? in vain:
Ah, youth is fled!
  A second blossom I but vainly crave:
The flower, that opes with peace to come,
  Is budding in the grave.

THE ADIEU.

LONE Lodge in the bend of the valley, farewel!

    Thou spot, ever dear to my view;

My anguish my bosom's forbidden to tell,

    While wandering I bid thee adieu.

Stain'd Rose-bud! thou once of my ballad the pride,

    Till proof brought thy canker to view;

Though heedlessly now thou hast roam'd from thy

      guide,

    I still wish thy foes may be few.

My love thou hast never yet known to deceive,

    I vow'd ever constant to be;

And thy faithful returns did as firmly believe,

    Till proof found a failing in thee.

Thou'rt lovely, I own it in many a sigh,

But what has such beauty to win?

The night-shade, it blossoms as fair to the eye,

That harbours dead poison within.

O Rosebud! thou subject of many a song,

Thy defilement's too plain to my view;

I love thee, but cannot forgive thee the wrong;

I hope, but it's vainly;—adieu!

Resolv'd never more to behold you again,

Or to visit the spot where you dwell,

My last look I'm leaving on Walkherd's lov'd plain,

My last vow I'm breathing—farewel!

SONGS AND BALLADS.

Clare, John, 1793 1864.

Poems descriptive of rural life and
peasant

UPON THE PLAIN.

A BALLAD.

———

Upon the plain there liv'd a swain,
  A flock his whole employ;
Unknown love's cares, and all its snares,
  To damp his humble joy.

Industry toils, while Fortune smiles,
  To bless him with increase;
Contentment made his humble trade
  A scene of health and peace.

But Cupid sly, whose jealous eye
   Envied his happiness,
With pointed darts and subtle arts
   Resolv'd on his distress.

Though first in vain he work'd his brain,
   Yet, practis'd in deceit,
Fresh schemes and plans were nigh his hands;
   And some were sure to hit.

In fatal hour he prov'd his power;
   A shepherd's form he's ta'en,
With crook and song he hums along,
   And thus accosts the swain:

" Go, friend," he cried, " to yonder side
   The hedge that bounds the plain,
For there a lamb has lost its dam,
   And bleats for help in vain."

Intent to start, his tender heart

    O'erlooks the subtle snare,

The swain's beguil'd, pleas'd Cupid smil'd,

    Fair Florimel was there.

The roses red her cheeks bespread,

    Her bosom's lily white;

To view her charms each bosom warms,

    Enraptur'd at the sight.

Her heaving breast, her slender waist,

    Her shape genteel and tall,

Her charms divine unrivall'd shine,

    Alike confess'd by all.

Beneath the shade, the lovely maid

    Lay shelter'd from the sun.

O luckless swain! go, fly the plain,

    Or stay and be undone.

For, ah! 'twas prov'd, by them that lov'd,
  She own'd a scornful eye;
Her pride was vain, the way to gain
  Her pity, was to die.

Stretch'd on the green, her beauty's seen
  To all advantage there;
To meet the breeze that fann'd the trees,
  Her snowy neck was bare.

She meets his view; sweet Peace, adieu!
  And pleasures known before:
He sighs, approves, admires, and loves;
  His heart's his own no more.

THE COUNTRY GIRL.

———

OH, dear! what fine thinkings beset me,
Since the young farmer yesterday met me,
To tell me for truth he would get me
    Some service more fitting in town ·
For he said 'twas a shame, and he swore too,
That I should be serv'd so, and more too,
And that he was vex'd o'er and o'er too,
    To see me so sadly run down.

When to thank him, for curtsey'ng I dropp'd me,
He said 'twas all foolish, and stopp'd me;
And into his arms, oh! he popp'd me,
    And crumpled my bonnet awry:

The tray sav'd the fall, till he mov'd it,

And this way and that way he shov'd it;

Good behaviour, he said, how he lov'd it,

   When maids were not foolish and shy.

Oh, dear! what fine thinkings beset me,

Since the young farmer promis'd, and met me,

Of what he would do and would get me,

   How my heart pittipatters about:

Though fear—none but fools make a trade on—

He swore when he saw what I play'd on,

" My word is my bond, pretty maiden!"

   Then why need I harbour a doubt?

Though the tale-clacking grass's foul staining

In my holiday clothes is remaining,

I ne'er shall go make a complaining,

   I've promise of better in town:

So Chub needn't come again croaking,

To maul one about, so provoking,

I know what is what, without joking,

    There's nought got by pleasing a clown.

PATTY OF THE VALE.

WHERE lonesome woodlands close surrounding

    Mark the spot a solitude,

And nature's uncheck'd scenes abounding

    Form a prospect wild and rude,

A cottage cheers the spot so glooming,

    Hid in the hollow of the dale,

Where, in youth and beauty blooming,

    Lives sweet Patty of the Vale.

Gay as the lambs her cot surrounding,
  Sporting wild the shades among,
O'er the hills and bushes bounding,
  Artless, innocent, and young,
Fresh, as blush of morning roses,
  Ere the mid-day suns prevail,
Fair, as lily-bud uncloses,
  Blooms sweet Patty of the Vale.

Low and humble though her station,
  Dress though mean she's doom'd to wear,
Few superiors in the nation
  With her beauty can compare.
What are riches ?—not worth naming,
  Though with some they may prevail;
Their's be choice of wealth proclaiming,
  Mine is Patty of the Vale.

Fools may fancy wealth and fortune

    Join to make a happy pair,

And for such the god importune,

    With full many a fruitless prayer:

I, their pride and wealth disdaining

    Should my humble hopes prevail,

Happy then, would cease complaining,

    Blest with Patty of the Vale.

SAD WAS THE DAY

SAD was the day when my Willy did leave me,

    Sad were the moments that wing'd him away;

And oh, most distressing, and most it did grieve me,

    To witness his looks while I begg'd him to stay.

It hurt him to think that in vain was I crying,

    Which I couldn't help, though I knew it so too;

The trumpets all sounding, the colours all flying,

    A soldier my Willy—my Willy must go.

The youths, never heeding to-morrow and danger,

    Kept laughing and toasting their girls o'er their
        beer;

But oh, my poor Willy, just like a lost stranger,

    Stood speechless among them, half dead as it
        were.

He kiss'd me—'twas all—not a word when he
        started,

    And oh, in his silence too much I could see,

He knew for a truth, and he knew, broken hearted,

    That kiss was the last he should ever give me.

FRIEND LUBIN.

FRIEND Lubin loves his Saturdays,

   That bring him rest on Sundays;

But *Whittler* loves contrary ways,

   And wishes all were Mondays.

The Labourer doats on welcome night

   To rest his weary limbs;

And Misses in the day delight,

   To shew their dressy whims.

But oh, the day and night to me,

   The Saturday or Monday,

1 care not which-a-way they be,

   Or working day or Sunday:

Oh no, I care not what they be,

　　Though night I most approve;

But oh, the day is dear to me,

　　That brings me to my love.

TO-DAY THE FOX MUST DIE.

A HUNTING SONG.

THE cock awakes the rosy dawn,

　　And tells approaching day,

While Reynard sneaks along the lawn

　　Belated with his prey:

Oh never think to find thy home,

　　But for thy safety fly;

The sportsman's long proclaim'd thy doom,

　　" To-day a Fox shall die."

The bugle blows, the sporting train
　　Swift mount the snorting steed,
Each fence defiance bids in vain
　　Their progress to impede;
The cover broke, they drive along,
　　And raise a jovial cry;
Each dog barks chorus to my song,
　　" To-day a Fox shall die."

Like lightning o'er the hills they sweep,
　　The readiest roads they go;
The five-barr'd gate with ease they leap:
　　Hark forward, tally ho!
The mist hangs on, and scents him strong,
　　The moisture makes it lie;
The woods re-echo to my song,
　　" This day the Fox must die."

Old Reynard finding shifts in vain,
　While hounds and horns pursue,
Now leaves the woods to try the plain,
　The bugle sounds a view:
Old Threadbrake gaily leads the throng;
　His bold unerring cry
Confirms the burthen of my song,
　" This day a Fox shall die."

His funeral knell the bugle blows,
　His end approaches near,
He reels and staggers as he goes,
　And drops his brush with fear:
More eager now they press along,
　And louder still the cry,
All join in chorus to my song,
　" To-day the Fox must die."

MY LAST SHILLING.

O DISMAL disaster! O troublesome lot!

What a heart-rending theme for my musing I've got:

Then pray what's the matter?—O friend, I'm not

willing,

The thought grieves me sore,

Now I'm driven to shore—

And must I then spend my last shilling, last shilling?

And must I then spend my last shilling?

O painful reflection! thou whole of my store,

That for these three months in my breeches I wore;

To spend thee, to spend thee, the thought turns me

chilling:

Oh, must I in spite

Of all reason, this night,

A farewel bid to my last shilling, last shilling,

A farewel bid to my last shilling?

How oft in my corner I've bother'd my pate,

First mourn'd at my shilling, and then at my fate,

To think the world's riches—though painful and
     killing,

    While I here endure

    The sad pain past a cure,

Of being drain'd to my very last shilling, last
    shilling,

Of being drain'd to my very last shilling.

O couldst thou but answer, dear whole of my store,

I'd ask thee a question: Thus friendless and poor,

'Tis whether thou wouldst to forsake me be willing?

Or whether it still

Would be more to thy will

To stay, and be call'd my last shilling, last shilling?

To stay, and be call'd my last shilling?

Thou source of reflection, my friend, and my all!

For tho' I'm left friendless thou stick'st to thy stall;

And through each vexing trouble seem'st cheery and

 willing:

 Thee to keep I'll contrive,

 For I'm sure I shan't thrive

If ever I spend such a shilling, a shilling,

If ever I spend such a shilling.

So still, old companion, stick true to the breeches,

And wear this old pocket thread-bare to its

 stitches;

For ever to keep thee I really am willing:

And who knows, but what thou

(Though I'm hard ashore now)

May turn out a lucky last shilling, last shilling,

May turn out a lucky last shilling ?

———◆———

HER I LOVE.

———

ROSE, in full blown blushes dyed,

    Pink, maturely spread,

Carnations, boasting all their pride

    Of melting white and red,

Are charms confess'd by every eye;

    But, ah! how faint they prove

To paint superior charms, when nigh

    The cheek of her I love.

Ripe cherry on its parent tree,

   With full perfection grac'd,

Red coral in its native sea,

   To all advantage plac'd;

What charms they boast the eye to please,

   And beauty to improve:

But, ah! all's lost, when match'd with these

   The lips of her I love.

The pulpy plum, when ripeness swells

   Its down-surrounding blue—

The dews besprent on heather bells,

   Reflecting brighter hue—

The azure sky, when stars appear

   Its blueness to improve,

Fade into dullest shades, when near

   The eyes of her I love.

Sweet is the blossom'd bean's perfume,

   By morning breezes shed;

And sweeter still the jonquil's bloom,

   When eve bedews its head;

The perfume sweet of pink and rose,

   And violet of the grove:

But ah! how sweeter far than those,

   The kiss of her I love.

MY LOVE, THOU ART A NOSEGAY SWEET.

My love, thou art a nosegay sweet,

   My sweetest flower I prove thee;

And pleas'd I pin thee to my breast,

   And dearly do I love thee.

And when, my nosegay, thou shalt fade,

    As sweet a flower thou'lt prove thee;

And as thou witherest on my breast,

    For beauty past I'll love thee.

And when, my nosegay, thou shalt die,

    And heaven's flower shalt prove thee;

My hopes shall follow to the sky,

    And everlasting love thee.

MY LOVE'S LIKE A LILY.

My love's like a lily, my love's like a rose,

My love's like a smile the spring mornings disclose;

And sweet as the rose, on her cheek her love glows,

    When sweetly she smileth on me:

But as cold as the snow of the lily, my rose
   Behaves to pretenders, whoever they be;
In vain higher stations their passions disclose,
   To win her affections from me.

My love's like a lily, my love's like a rose,
My love's like the smile the spring mornings dis-
      close;
And fair as the lily, and sweet as the rose,
   My love's beauty bloometh to me:
And smiles of more pleasure my heart only knows,
   To think that pretenders, whoever they be,
But vainly their love and their passions disclose;
   My love remains constant to me.

TRUE LOVE.

TRUE love, the virgin's first fond passion,
　　How blest the swain to prove it!
Should Hymen snatch the lucky hour,
　　No power on earth can move it.

When death such loving hearts divides,
　　And love on earth is blasting;
Firm fix'd the hope in heaven remains,
　　Where love is everlasting.

THE FIRST OF MAY.

A BALLAD.

FAIR blooms the rose upon the green,
   Pretending to excel;
But who another rose has seen,
   A different tale can tell.
The morning smiles, the lark's begun
   To welcome in the May:
Be cloudless, skies! look out, bright sun!
   And haste my love away.

Though graceful round the maidens move,
   That join the rural ball,
Soon shall they own my absent love
   The rival of them all.

Go, wake your shepherdess, ye lambs!
    And murmur her delay:
Chide her neglect, ye hoarser dams!
    And call my love away.

Ye happy swains, with each a bride,
    Were but the angel there,
While slighted maids despair'd and sigh'd,
    You'd court th' unequall'd fair.
Dry up, ye dews! nor threat'ning hing,
    To soil her best array ·
Ye birds! with double vigour sing,
    And urge my love away.

Welcome, sun! the dews are fled,
    The lark has rais'd his song;
The daisy nauntles up its head,—
    Why waits my love so long?

As flowrets fade, the pleasures bloom,

  All hastening to decay :

The day steals on, and showers may come :

  This instant haste away.

What now, ye fearful cringing sheep !

  Who meets your wondering eyes?

What makes you 'neath the maples creep,

  In homaging surprise?

No ladies tread our humble green:

  Ah! welcome wonders, hail!

I witness your mistaken queen

  Is Patty of the Vale.

SONNETS.

THE SETTING SUN.

THIS scene, how beauteous to a musing mind,
   That now swift slides from my enchanting view;
The Sun sweet setting yon far hills behind,
   In other worlds his visits to renew:
What spangled glories all around him shine;
   What nameless colours, cloudless and serene,
(A heav'nly prospect, brightest in decline,)
   Attend his exit from this lovely scene.
So sets the Christian's sun, in glories clear;
So shines his soul at his departure here:
   No clouding doubts, nor misty fears arise,
To dim Hope's golden rays of being forgiven;
   His Sun, sweet setting in the clearest skies,
In safe assurance wings the soul to heaven.

THE PRIMROSE.

WELCOME, pale Primrose! starting up between.
  Dead matted leaves of ash and oak, that strew
  The every lawn, the wood, and spinney through,
Mid creeping moss and ivy's darker green;
  How much thy presence beautifies the ground:
How sweet thy modest, unaffected pride
Glows on the sunny bank, and wood's warm side.
  And where thy fairy flowers in groups are found,
The school-boy roams enchantedly along,
  Plucking the fairest with a rude delight:
While the meek shepherd stops his simple song,
  To gaze a moment on the pleasing sight;
O'erjoy'd to see the flowers that truly bring
The welcome news of sweet returning Spring.

CHRISTIAN FAITH.

WHAT antidote or charm on earth is found,
  To alleviate or soften fate's decree?
To fearless enter on that dark profound,
  Where life emerges in eternity?

Wisdom, a rushlight vainly boasting power
  To cheer the terrors sin's first visit gave,
Denies existence at that dreadful hour,
  And shrinks in horror from a gaping grave.

O Christianity, thou charm divine!
That firmness, faith, and last resource is thine:
  With thee the Christian joys to lose his breath,
Nor dreads to find his mortal strength decay;
  But, dear in friendship, shakes the hand of Death,
And hugs the pain that gnaws his life away.

THE MOON.

How sweet the Moon extends her cheering ray
   To damp the terrors of the darksome night,
Guiding the lonely traveller on his way,
   Pointing the path that leads his journey right.
   Hail! welcome! blessing! to thy silver light,
That charms dull night, and makes its horrors gay.
   So shines the Gospel to the Christian's soul;
So by its light and inspiration given,
   He (spite of sin and Satan's black control)
Through all obstructions steers his course to heaven.
   So did the Saviour his design pursue,
That we, unworthy sinners, might be bless'd;
   So suffer'd death. its terrors to subdue,
And made the grave a wish'd-for place of rest.

THE GIPSY'S EVENING BLAZE.

To me how wildly pleasing is that scene
  Which doth present, in evening's dusky hour,
A group of Gipsies, centred on the green,
  In some warm nook where Boreas has no pow'r;
Where sudden starts the quivering blaze behind
  Short, shrubby bushes, nibbled by the sheep,
  That mostly on these short sward pastures keep;
Now lost, now seen, now bending with the wind:
And now the swarthy sybil kneels reclin'd;
  With proggling stick she still renews the blaze,
  Forcing bright sparks to twinkle from the flaze.
When this I view, the all-attentive mind
  Will oft exclaim (so strong the scene pervades),
  " Grant me this life, thou spirit of the shades !

A SCENE.

THE Landscape's stretching view, that opens wide,
  With dribbling brooks, and river's wider floods,
  And hills, and vales, and darksome lowering
    woods,
With green of varied hues, and grasses pied;
  The low brown cottage in the shelter'd nook;
The steeple, peeping just above the trees
Whose dangling leaves keep rustling in the breeze;
  And thoughtful shepherd bending o'er his hook;
And maidens stripp'd, haymaking too, appear;
  And Hodge a whistling at his fallow plough;
  And herdsman hallooing to intruding cow:
All these, with hundreds more, far off and near,
  Approach my sight; and please to such excess,
  That language fails the pleasure to express.

TO THE GLOW WORM.

TASTEFUL Illumination of the night,
  Bright scatter'd, twinkling star of spangled earth!
Hail to the nameless colour'd dark-and-light,
  The witching nurse of thy illumin'd birth.
In thy still hour how dearly I delight
  To rest my weary bones, from labour free;
In lone spots, out of hearing, out of sight,
  To sigh day's smother'd pains; and pause on thee,
  Bedecking dangling brier and ivied tree,
Or diamonds tipping on the grassy spear;
  Thy pale-fac'd glimmering light I love to see,
Gilding and glistering in the dew-drop near:
  O still-hour's mate! my easing heart sobs free,
While tiny bents low bend with many an added tear.

K

THE ANT.

THOU little Insect, infinitely small,
  What curious texture marks thy minute frame;
How seeming large thy foresight, and withal,
  Thy labouring talents not unworthy fame,
To raise such monstrous hills along the plain,
  Larger than mountains, when compar'd with thee:
To drag the crumb dropp'd by the village swain,
  Huge size to thine, is strange, indeed, to me.
But that great instinct which foretels the cold,
  And bids to guard 'gainst winter's wasteful power,
Endues this mite with cheerfulness to hold
  Its toiling labours through the sultry hour:
So that same soothing power, in misery,
Cheers the poor pilgrim to eternity.

TO HOPE.

AH, smiling cherub! cheating Hope, adieu!

No more I'll listen to your pleasing themes;

No more your flattering scenes with joy renew,

For ah, I've found them all delusive dreams ·

Yes, mere delusions all; therefore, adieu!

No more shall you this aching heart beguile;

No more your fleeting joys will I pursue,

That mock'd my sorrows when they seem'd to

smile,

And flatter'd tales that never will be true:

Tales, only told to aggravate distress

And make me at my fate the more repine,

By whispering joys I never can possess,

And painting scenes that never can be mine.

A WINTER SCENE.

———

HAIL, Scenes of desolation and despair,
  Keen Winter's overbearing sport and scorn!
Torn by his rage, in ruins as you are,
  To me more pleasing than a summer's morn
Your shatter'd state appears;—despoil'd and bare,
  Stripp'd of your clothing, naked and forlorn:—
Yes, winter's havock! wretched as you shine,
  Dismal to others as your fate may seem,
Your fate is pleasing to this heart of mine,
  Your wildest horrors I the most esteem:
The ice-bound floods that still with rigour freeze,
  The snow-cloth'd valley, and the naked tree,
These sympathising scenes my heart can please,
  Distress is their's—and they resemble me.

EVENING.

Now glaring daylight's usher'd to a close;
  And nursing Eve her soothing care renews,
To welcome weary labour to repose,
  And cherish nature with reviving dews.
Hail, cooling sweets! that breathe so sweetly here;
  Hail, lovely Eve! whose hours so lovely prove;
Thy silent calm! to solitude so dear;
  And oh, this darkness! dearer still to love.
Now the fond lover seeks thy silent plains,
  And with his charmer in fond dalliance strays,
Vowing his love, and telling jealous pains
  Which doubtful fancies in their absence raise.
Ah! though such pleasures centre not in me,
I love to wander and converse with thee.

TO THE WINDS.

HAIL, gentle Winds! I love your murmuring sound;
 The willows charm me, wavering to and fro;
And oft I stretch me on the daisied ground,
 To see you crimp the wrinkled flood below:
Delighted more as brisker gusts succeed,
 And give the landscape round a sweeter grace,
Sweeping in shaded waves the ripening mead,
 Puffing their rifled fragrance in my face.
Painters of Nature! ye are doubly dear;
 Her children dearly love your whispering charms:
Ah, ye have murmur'd sweet to many an ear
 That now lies dormant in death's icy arms;
And at this moment many a weed ye wave,
That hides the bard in his forgotten grave.

NATIVE SCENES.

O NATIVE Scenes, for ever, ever dear!
  So blest, so happy as I here have been,
  So charm'd with nature in each varied scene,
To leave you all is cutting and severe.
  Ye hawthorn bushes that from winds would
      screen,
Where oft I've shelter'd from a threaten'd shower;
In youth's past bliss, in childhood's happy hour,
  Ye woods I've wandered, seeking out the nest;
Ye meadows gay that rear'd me many a flower,
  Where, pulling cowslips, I've been doubly blest,
Humming gay fancies as I pluck'd the prize:
  Oh, fate unkind! beloved scenes, adieu!
Your vanish'd pleasures crowd my swimming eyes,
  And make the wounded heart to bleed anew.

TO A FAVOURITE TREE.

OLD, favourite Tree! art thou too fled the scene?
   Could not thy 'clining age the axe delay,
And let thee stretch thy shadows o'er the green,
   And let thee die in picturesque decay?
What hadst thou done to meet a tyrant's frown?
   Small value was the ground on which thou stood;
But gain's rude rage it was that cut thee down,
   And dragg'd thee captive from thy native wood.
So gay in summer as thy boughs were dress'd,
   So soft, so cool, as then thy leaves did wave;
I knew thee then, and knowing am distress'd:
   And like as Friendship leaning o'er the grave,
Loving ye all, ye trees, ye bushes, dear,
I wander where you stood, and shed my bosom-tear.

APPROACH OF SPRING.

SWEET are the omens of approaching Spring,
  When gay the elder sprouts her winged leaves;
When tootling robins carol-welcomes sing,
  And sparrows chelp glad tidings from the eaves.
What lovely prospects wait each wakening hour,
  When each new day some novelty displays;
How sweet the sun-beam melts the crocus flower,
  Whose borrow'd pride shines dizen'd in his rays:
Sweet, new-laid hedges flush their tender greens;
Sweet peep the arum-leaves their shelter screens;
  Ah! sweet are all which I'm denied to share:
Want's painful hindrance sticks me to her stall;—
  But still Hope's smiles unpoint the thorns of Care,
Since Heaven's eternal Spring is free for all.

SUMMER.

———

THE oak's slow-opening leaf, of deepening hue,
  Bespeaks the power of Summer once again;
While many a flower unfolds its charms to view,
  To glad the entrance of his sultry reign.
Where peep the gaping, speckled cuckoo-flowers,
  Sweet is each rural scene she brings to pass;
Prizes to rambling school-boys' vacant hours,
  Tracking wild searches through the meadow grass:
The meadow-sweet taunts high its showy wreath,
And sweet the quaking grasses hide beneath.
  Ah, 'barr'd from all that sweetens life below,
Another Summer still my eyes can see
  Freed from this scorn and pilgrimage of woe,
To share the Seasons of Eternity.

THE RIVER GWASH.

WHERE winding Gwash whirls round its wildest
    scene,
  On this romantic bend I sit me down;
On that side view the meadow's smoothing green,
    Edg'd with the peeping hamlet's checquering
    brown;
  Here the steep bank, as dropping headlong down;
While glides the stream a silver streak between,
  As glide the shaded clouds along the sky,
Bright'ning and deep'ning, losing as they're seen,
In light and shade: to where old willows lean,
  Thus their broad shadow runs the river by,
With tree and bush replete, a wilder'd scene,
  And moss and ivy speckling on my eye.
Oh, thus while musing wild, I'm doubly blest,
My woes unheeding, and my heart at rest.

TO RELIGION.

———

THOU sacred light, that right from wrong discerns;
   Thou safeguard of the soul, thou heaven on earth;
Thou undervaluer of the world's concerns,
   Thou disregarder of its joys and mirth;
Thou only home the houseless wanderers have;
   Thou prop by which the pilgrim's woes are borne;
Thou solace of the lonely hermit's cave,
   That beds him down to rest on fate's sharp thorn;
Thou only hope to sorrow's bosom given;
   Thou voice of mercy when the weary call;
Thou faith extending to thy home in heaven;
   Thou peace, thou rest, thou comfort, all in all:
O sovereign good! on thee all hopes depend,
Till thy grand source unfolds its realizing end.

ANXIETY

ONE, o'er heaths wandering in a pitch dark night,
  Making to sounds that hope some village near;
Hermit, retreating to a chinky light,
  Long lost in winding cavern dark and drear;
  A slave, long banish'd from his country dear,
By freedom left to seek his native plains;
  A soldier, absent many a long, long year,
In sight of home ere he that comfort gains;
A thirsty labouring wight, that wistful strains
  O'er the steep hanging bank to reach the stream;
A hope, delay so lingeringly detains,
  We still on point of its disclosure seem:
These pictures weakly 'semble to the eye
A *faint* existence of Anxiety.

EXPECTATION.

———

WHEN Expectation in the bosom heaves,
　　What longing, anxious views disturb the mind;
What fears, what hopes, distrust and then believe
　　That something which the heart expects to find:
How the poor prisoner, ere he's doom'd to die,
　　Within his gloomy cell of dreary woe,
How does he watch, with Expectation's eye,
　　The lingering, long suspense of fate to know.
Alas, poor soul! though different bonds confine;
The walls his prison is, the world is mine:
　　So do I turn my weary eyes above,
So do I look and sigh for peace to come,
　　So do I long the grave's dark end to prove,
And anxious wait my long, long journey home.

TO MY OATEN REED.

THOU warble wild, of rough, rude melody,
    How oft I've woo'd thee, often thrown thee by;
In many a doubtful rapture touching thee,
    Waking thy rural notes in many a sigh:
    Fearing the wise, the wealthy, proud and high,
Would scorn as vain thy lowly extasy;
    Deeming presumptuous thy uncultur'd themes.
Thus vainly courting Taste's unblemish'd eye,
    To list a simple Labourer's artless dreams,
    Haply I wander into wide extremes.
But O thou sweet, wild-winding rhapsody,
    Thou jingling charm that dost my heart control;
I take thee up to smother many a sigh,
    And lull the throbbings of a woe-worn soul.

CRAZY NELL.

A TRUE STORY.

———

THE sun lowly sinking behind the far trees,

And, crossing the path, humming home were the
    bees;

And darker and darker it grew by degrees,

    And crows they flock'd quawking to rest:

When, unknown to her parents, Nell slove on her
    hat,

And o'er the fields hurried—scarce knew she for
    what;

But her sweetheart, in taking advantage and that,

    Had kiss'd, and had promis'd the best.

Poor maidens ! of husbands so much they conceit,

The daisy scarce touch'd rose unhurt from her feet,

So eager she hasten'd her lover to meet,

  As to make him to wait was unjust;

On the wood, dim discover'd, she fixed her eyes—

Such a queer spot to meet in—suspicions might rise;

But the fond word " a sweetheart " such goodness

  implies,

  Ah, who would a lover distrust!

More gloomy and darker—black clouds hung the

  wind,

Far objects diminish'd before and behind,

More narrow and narrow the circle declin'd,

  And silence reign'd awfully round,

When Nelly within the wood-riding sat down;

She listen'd, and lapp'd up her arms in her gown;

Far, far from her cottage, and far from the town,

  And her sweetheart not yet to be found.

The minutes seem'd hours—with impatience she
    heard
The flap of a leaf, and the twit of a bird;
The least little trifle that whisper'd or stirr'd,
    Hope pictur'd her lover as nigh ·
When wearied with sitting, she wander'd about,
And open'd the wood-gate, and gave a look out;
And fain would have halloo'd, but Fear had a doubt
    That thieves might be lurking hard by.

Far clocks count eleven—" He won't be long now,"
Her anxious hopes whisper'd—hoarse wav'd the
    wood bough ;
—" He heeds not my fears, or he's false to his vow !"
    Poor Nelly sat doubtful, and sigh'd :
The man who had promis'd her husband to be,
And to wed on the morrow—her friends all could see
That a good-for-nought sort of a fellow was he,
    And they hop'd nothing worse might betide.

At length, as in fear, slowly tapp'd the wood-gate:

'Twas Ben!—she complain'd so long painful to wait.

Deep design hung his looks, he but mumbled "'Tis

    late,"

    And pass'd her, and bid her come on.

The mind plainly pictures that *night-hour* of dread,

In the midst of a wood! where the trees over head

The darkness increased—a dungeon they spread,

    And the clock at the moment toll'd one!

Nell fain would have forc'd, as she follow'd, some

    chat;

And trifled, on purpose, with this thing and that;

And complain'd of the dew-dropping spoiling her

    hat;

    But nothing Ben's silence would break.

Extènsive the forest, the roads to and fro,

And this way and that way, above and below,

As crossing the ridings, as winding they go —

    " Ah! what road or way can he seek?"

Her eye, ever watchful, now caught an alarm;

Lights gleam, and tools tinkle, as if nigh a farm:

"O don't walk so fast, Ben—I'm fearful of harm!"

    She said, and shrugg'd closer behind.

"That light's from my house!" 'twas the first word

    she caught

From his lips, since he through the dark wood had

    her brought.

A house in a wood! Oh, good God! what a thought;

    What sensations then rush'd on her mind!

The things, which her friends and her neighbours had

    said,

Afresh at that moment all jump'd in her head;

And mistrust, for the first time, now fill'd her with

    dread:

    And as she approach'd, she could see

How better, for her, their advice to have ta'en;

And she wish'd to herself then she had—but in vain:

—A heap of fresh mould, and a spade, she saw plain,

    And a lantern tied up to a tree.

" Here they come ! " a voice whispers ;—" Haste !
 put out the light."
" No: dig the grave deeper !"—" Very dark is the
 night."
Slow mutterings mingled.—Oh, dismal the sight !
 —The fate of poor Nelly was plain.
Fear chill'd through her heart—but Hope whisper'd
 her—Fly !
Chance seiz'd on the moment, a wind-gust blew high,
She slipt in the thicket—he turn'd not his eye,
 And the grave-diggers waited in vain.

At that fearful moment, so dreadfully dark,
How welcome the song of the shepherd, or lark;
How cheery to hearken, and hear the dog bark,
 As through the dark wood she fled fast :
But, horror of horrors, all nature was hush !
Not a sound was there heard—save a blackbird, or
 thrush,
That, started from sleep, flusker'd out of the bush,
 Which her brushing clothes shook as they past.

Fear now truly pictur'd: she ne'er turu'd her head
Either this way or that way—straight forward she
    fled;
And Fancy, still hearing the horrors with dread,
    On faster and fearfuller stole.
The matted leaves rustle—the boughs swiftly part,
Her hands and her face with the brambles did
    smart;
But, oh! the worst anguish was felt at her heart,—
    Ben's unkindness struck death to her soul.

Now glimmering lighter the forest appears,
And Hope, the sweet comforter, soften'd her fears;
Light and liberty, darkness! thy horror endears;
    Great bliss did the omen impart:
The forest, its end, and its terrors gone by,
She breath'd the free air, and she saw the blue sky;
Her own fields she knew—to her home did she
    fly,
    And great was the joy of her heart.

Oh, prospect endearing! the village to view,

The morn sweet appearing,—and gay the cock crew,

When, mangled by brambles and dabbled in dew,

    She gave a loud rap at the door:

The parents in raptures wept over their child;

She mutter'd her terrors—her eyes rolled wild—

" They dig the grave deeper!—Your Nelly's be-
guil'd!"

    She said, and she siled on the floor.

Poor Nell soon recover'd; but, ah! to her cost,

Her sense and her reason for ever were lost:

And scorch'd by the summer, and chill'd by the frost,

    A maniac, restless and wild,

Now crazy Nell rambles; and still she will weep,

And, fearless, at night into hovels will creep.—

Fond parents! alas, their affliction is deep,

    And vainly they comfort their child.

GLOSSARY.

L

GLOSSARY.

Bangs, *v. n.* moves with violence.

Battled, *part.* bespattered with mud.

Battered, *v. n.* fought his way.

Beetling, *part.* striking with a heavy wooden mallet, called a beetle. See Folds.

Bevering, *adj.* drinking, (from Bevere, Ital. to drink: whence Beverage, and the Beaver of a helmet.)

Bird-boy, *sub.* a boy who frightens birds from the corn.

Booing and mooing, *part.* expressing the noise of cattle when they bellow.

Bum, *v. n.* to rush with a murmuring sound. (*Dict.* Boom.)

Chaps, *sub.* young fellows.

Chelp, *v.* a. to chirp, or make a chattering noise like a bird.

Clammed, *part.* exhausted for want of food.

'Clining, for declining.

Conceit, *v. n.* to think extravagantly.

Crampt, *adj.* limited, confined.

Crumbles, *sub.* crumbs.

Crumping, *adj.* crushing, with a low, abrupt noise.

Culling, *part* for culled, chosen.

Cumbergrounds, *sub.* a name for useless trees. " Cut it down, why cumbereth it the ground."

Dinged on the nose,—taunted, reproved.

Dinner-tin, a tin vessel containing his dinner.

Dithering, *part.* shaking with cold.—(*Ash's Dict.* Didder.)

Drowking, *part.* drooping, faint with drouth.

Eggs on, *v. n.* urges forward.

'Fex, a petty oath.

Flaze, *sub.* a smoky flame,—by contraction probably of *flash* and *haze.*

Flops, *v. a.* outspreads, as it were broad wings.

Fluskered, *v n.* flew with sudden and disordered motion.

Folds, *sub.* inclosures made with hurdles, wherein sheep are penned at night.

Gad, *sub.* the gad-fly.

Gie, for give.

'Gin, for begin.

Glowered, *v. n.* stared. (So BURNS.)

Goss, *sub.* gorse, furze.

Hing, *v. a.* to hang. (So CHAUCER.)

Hob, *sub.* the ledge or shelf of a fire-grate.

Kerchup,—the noise of partridges calling to each other.

'Lotted, for allotted.

Lump away, *v. n* to beat with a heavy sound.

Lunge, *v. n.* to lurch, to hide, to skulk.

Matey, *sub.* for mate.

Matty, matted,—twisted, interwoven.

Mauls, *v. a.* rudely pushes.

'Minds, for reminds.

Mounting, *part.* equipping.

Mulls, *sub.* the name by which milk-maids call their cows.

Mun, *v n.* must.

Nappy, *sub.* ale.

Nauntles, *v. n.* meekly elevates.

'Neath, for beneath.

'Nighted, for benighted.

Palms, *sub.* the English palm, or sallow.

Pinks, *v a.* imbues with a pink colour.

Pint, *v.* a to drink a pint of ale.

'Plaining, for complaining.

'Prehensions, for apprehensions.

Proggling, *adj.* meddling, poking.

Quawking, *part.* the noise of crows, croaking, cawing.

Ragg'd muffins, *sub* raggamuffins.

Ridings, *sub.* the broad green-sward roads which intersect a wood.

Roll, *sub.* a large, heavy wooden roller for breaking clods.

Rocking, *part.* walking with alternate sideway motion.

Scrigg'd, *v a.* forced, or squeezed.

Searches, *sub.* researches.

'Semble, for resemble.

Shool, *v. a.* to carry for a pretence.

'Sides, for besides

Siled, *v. n.* fainted, sunk gradually.

Slive, *v. n.* to creep about, (*Ash's Dict.*) to do any thing slyly.

Slove, *præt.* of slive,—whence sloven.

Sloomy, *adj.* dully,—perhaps a contraction of *slow* and *gloomy.*

Snifting and snutting, *part.* snuffing.

Soodles, *v. n.* goes unwillingly.

Spinney, *sub.* a natural wood,—a hedge-row thicket,—a young
    coppice. (*Ash's Dict.*)

Stubs, *sub.* stubble.

Sprouts, *v. a.* puts forth.

Stall, *sub.* a shed, a temporary hut.

Standard, *adj.* trees or plants that grow unsupported.

Streaked, *part.* stretched. So used by CHAPMAN.

Swaliest, *adj.* coolest. (Bailey's *Dict.*)

Swish, *sub.* a dash, as of water falling.

Taunts, *v. a.* tosses, as if scornfully.

Tint, a contraction of " *it is not.*"

Tinty, *adj.* tinted.

Tools, *sub.* farming utensils.

Tootling, *adj.* the noise made with the tongue in playing on the flute.

Unmatch'd, *adj.* used here for *unequally matched.*

'Veigled, for inveigled.

'Venturer, for adventurer.

Waterpudge, *sub.* or podge, a puddle. (*Johnson's Dict.*)

Wealed, *præt.* of weal, to raise marks on the skin with a whip.

Whanged, *præt.* threw down with violence.

Witchen, *sub.* quick-beam, or quicken-tree. (See *Ash's Dict.*) The quick-beam, wild sorb, or witchen, is a species of wild ash. (*Evelyn's Sylva.*)

Won't,—contraction of " *will not.*"

THE END.

T. Miller, Printer, Noble Street, Cheapside, London.

CHRONOLOGY

1792   Shelley born.

1793   John Clare born at Helpston, 13 July. His twin sister dies.

1794   Blake's *Songs of Experience*. Erasmus Darwin's *Zoönomia*.

1795   Keats born. Speenhamland system of poor relief introduced.

1796   Death of Burns.

1797   Bewick's *History of British Birds*.

1798   Battle of the Nile. *Lyrical Ballads*.

1799   Religious Tract Society founded.

1800   Bloomfield's *The Farmer's Boy*. Death of Cowper. *Preface to Lyrical Ballads*.

1802   Scott's *Minstrelsy of the Scottish Border*. Bloomfield's *Rural Tales*.

1803   Hayley's *Life of Cowper*.

1804   Napoleon proclaimed Emperor.

1805   Clare befriends Mary Joyce at school in Glinton. Cary's translation of Dante's *Inferno*. Battle of Trafalgar (21 October).

1805–9 Clare worked as an agricultural labourer.

1806   Roscoe's *The Butterfly's Ball and Grasshopper's Feast*. Byron's *Fugitive Pieces*.

1807   Kirke White's *Remains*.

1808   Byron sails for the Mediterranean.

1809   Battle of Corunna. Enclosure Act for Helpston. Clare renews friendship with Mary Joyce.

1810   Crabbe's *The Borough*.

1810–13 Clare works at different jobs—a gardener at Burghley House, a militia recruit, a gang-labourer, a harvester.

1811   Luddite Riots. Bloomfield's *The Banks of Wye*.

1812   Byron's *Childe Harold* (I and II).

1813   Coleridge's *Remorse*.

1814   Cary completes his translation of Dante's *Divina Commedia*.

1814–18 Clare works at Helpston, Bridge Casterton, and Pickworth. Courts first Elizabeth Newbon and later Martha ('Patty') Turner. Issues in 1817 a proposal for publishing by subscription which catches the attention of Edward Drury, John Taylor's cousin.

1815   Waterloo. Napoleon exiled to St Helena. Byron's *Hebrew Melodies*.

1816   Shelley's *Alastor*.

1817   Keats's *Poems* published by Taylor and Hessey, who were to become Clare's publishers.

1818   Keats's *Endymion* published by Taylor and Hessey.

1819   Clare meets Taylor, who agrees to publish his poems.

1820   Publication of *Poems Descriptive of Rural Life and Scenery*. Marries 'Patty'. Clare visits London for the first time.

1821   *Poems Descriptive*, fourth edition. *The Village Minstrel and other Poems*. Taylor acquires the *London Magazine*. Death of Keats.

1822   Death of Shelley.

1822–4 Clare meets prominent literary figures during his visits to London. Writes 'The Parish'. Increasing anxiety and illness.

1823   Death of Octavius Gilchrist. Elizabeth Kent's *Flora Domestica*.

1824   Death of Byron. First number of Alaric Watt's *Literary Souvenir*. Taylor withdraws from the *London Magazine*.

1825   Taylor and Hessey dissolve their partnership. Cunningham's *Songs of Scotland, Ancient and Modern*. Death of Lord Radstock.

1825–6 Clare writes imitations of older poets. Prolific output.

1826   Hone's *Every-Day Book*.

1827   Publication of *The Shepherd's Calendar, with Village Stories and Other Poems* (written in 1824—by 1829 only 400 copies sold).

1828   Lockhart's *Life of Burns*. Clare visits London for relief of depression. Writes 'Pleasures of Spring'. Does field-work until 1831.

1829   Hogg's *The Shepherd's Calendar*. Tennyson's *Timbuctoo*.

1830   Publication of Dr Matthew Allen's *Cases of Insanity*. Moore's *Life of Byron*. Captain Swing Riots. Clare writes 'Hue and Cry'.

1831   Ebenezer Elliott's *Corn Law Rhymes*.

1832   Reform Act. Moves to Northborough to a cottage provided by Earl Fitzwilliam. Clare writes 'The Flitting'.

1833–4 Clare, planning to publish *The Midsummer Cushion*, meets endless delays.

1834   Poor Law Amendment Act.

1835   Publication of *The Rural Muse*, which is sympathetically received and sells reasonably well.

1836   Suffers lapses of memory and delusions.

1837   Publication of Dr Matthew Allen's *Classification of the Insane*. Clare enters High Beach as a voluntary patient. Accession of Queen Victoria.

1838–41 Clare treated by Dr Allen and improves physically but not mentally.

1841   Writes 'Child Harold' and 'Don Juan'. Escapes from Allen's (July), walks home to Northborough, and is removed to Northampton Asylum (December).

2–64   Clare spends his remaining years in Northampton Asylum.

W. F. Knight appointed House Steward, Northampton Asylum.

Death of Thomas Inskip and of Peter De Wint.

W. F. Knight leaves Northampton for Birmingham.

Clare dies at Northampton, 20 May, aged 70. Taylor dies 5 July.

W. B. Yeats born. Martin's *Life of John Clare* published.

readers who have read his poetry and prose for simple pleasure. T[...]
that pleasure we hope that this volume will add.

Acknowledgements

Scholars are helpless without librarians—and so we want to t[...]
the librarians and archivists who worked with us. Authors are o[...]
the mercy of their publishers—ours were very merciful to us. [...]
are often obliged to travel widely in search of their materials.
come to appreciate the hospitality and understanding of their fri[...]
Eric Robinson wishes to thank Bruce Bailey, Ian and Do[...]
Bowman, Sara and Jim Currie, Isabelle and George Deacon, Mar[...]
and Basil Mitchell, Anthea and Robert Morton Saner, and Edwar[...]
Storey. For helpful conversation he also wishes to thank Margaret
Grainger and Mark Storey.

David Powell wishes to thank The British Academy and its Small
Grants Research Fund in the Humanities, the Leverhulme Trust, and
the East Midlands Arts for financial assistance during the preparation
of this work. He is also grateful for the help of his wife Margaret, who
as always put up with a lot of disruption, and to Mrs Irene Butcher,
who willingly typed a large part of the manuscript.

We wish to thank The Carl and Lily Pforzheimer Foundation, Inc.
and The Carl H. Pforzheimer Library for permission to print *To the
Winds*, *Autumn* ('Syren of sullen moods and fading hues'), *The
Eternity of Nature*, *The Mores*, *The Flitting* and four prose pieces, [*Life
Peerages*], [*The Poor Man* Versus *the Rich Man*], [*Grammar*], and
[*Letter to William Hone*]; The Pierpont Morgan Library for *Rural
Morning*, *Rural Evening*, *Rustic Fishing*, *Sunday Walks*, *The Fate of
Genius*, *Winter* ('From huddling nights embrace how chill'); the
Henry W. and Albert A. Berg Collection, The New York Public
Library, Astor, Lenox and Tilden Foundations for *Song* ('A seaboy on
the giddy mast'), *Song* ('The daiseys golden eye'), *Song* ('The autumns
come again').

CPSIA information can be obtained at www.ICGtesting.com
Printed in the USA
BVOW11s1224090116

432288BV00020B/273/P

9 781331 384946